IMPLEMENTING

M R P I I

The Core of Manufacturing ERP

Sam Graham

authorHOUSE®

AuthorHouse™
1663 Liberty Drive
Bloomington, IN 47403
www.authorhouse.com
Phone: 1-800-839-8640

Published by AuthorHouse   02/23/2012

ISBN: 978-1-4678-8993-3 (sc)
ISBN: 978-1-4678-8992-6 (e)

Contents

1. Introduction and Brief History

When I sat down to write this book the first thing that I had to ask myself was whether I should write a book for newcomers to MRPII or for experienced users. After much thought, I decided that the answer was both. "How is that going to work?" I hear you ask. Surely the two will be coming at things from different angles? Newcomers will want to know the basics but seasoned practitioners will be looking to take their knowledge to the next level.

That is true, and certainly there is much in this book that is aimed at those who are coming to ERP/MRPII for the first time, but there are reasons why people who know enough to write a book such as this should read it instead. For one; in writing this book, I remembered things that I had long since, if not forgotten, at least pushed to the back of my mind in order to make way for new knowledge. Sometimes it is good to be reminded of what we know.

Another reason is that all of us know things that we believe to be true. We were taught them by people who were expert and knowledgeable. I know the formula for calculating the volume of a cylinder, for example. I trusted the school teacher who taught me it and, to this day, I have never doubted it or challenged it. But when I came to write things down, I realised that, if I said verbally something that was wrong, time would forgive me (and I could even deny it!). Writing something down and having it published, however, sets statements in stone so I had to be sure that I was right; especially when I found myself writing something that challenges received wisdom. People who know and understand MRP & MRPII will therefore be surprised by some of the things that I say in this book; such as:

- Accurate purchasing lead times are not important (see section 4.2), and
- Incomplete bills of material **should** be entered to the system (see section 4.6).

Feel free to disagree with me. In all the years that I have been educating and training in this field, I have never demanded that people agree with me. All that I have ever asked is that, if they do disagree, they understand why they disagree: that they think things through in their own mind and not just repeat some dusty mantra. I do not set out deliberately in this book to confront or challenge. I am just putting thirty years of experience down on paper in the belief that it may be of use to a newcomer and that, if an experienced user learns just one new thing from this book, it will have been worth the purchase price: in the world of manufacturing, one new idea sometimes can be enough to move mountains.

To specify the areas that this book is trying to cover, then, let's briefly summarise:

MRP (or to give it it's full name, Materials Requirements Planning); being a system that takes demands for products, calculates (generally by use of a Bill of Material) the requirements of sub-assemblies and raw materials necessary for their production and, through comparison with existing stocks and orders, recommends the actions necessary for the fulfilment of those requirements.

MRPII (Manufacturing Resource Planning); being MRP plus functionality in related areas, such as:

- Works Order Processing
- Purchase Order Processing
- Sales Order Processing
- Costing

And additionally the following modules that will not be explored in this book:

- Nominal (General) Ledger
- Accounts Payable (Purchase Ledger)
- Accounts Receivable (Sales Ledger)

as well as the plethora of other modules that are necessary in an efficient and effective manufacturing organisation. My not naming them all here does not suggest that they are not important, indeed vital in some companies: merely that they are not universally used. For example; Engineering Change Control is vital in some companies (such as those in aerospace) but is virtually ignored in others. Likewise, capacity planning and scheduling are critical in some industries but not in others. For example, in process industries, where the same product is produced on the same line each and every day, capacity planning is essential but capacity scheduling is largely irrelevant.

ERP (Enterprise Resource Planning) then adds most of the other things that companies need; such as CRM (Customer Relationship Management), payroll, personnel management etc. These are specialist areas in their own right and would merely detract from the MRP/MRPII message if addressed here.

With attention now turning to ERP, many manufacturing companies are forgetting that MRP and MRPII provide the foundations on which that grander system sits. If you are trying to run a manufacturing ERP system without getting MRP/MRPII to work, you are trying to run your Ferrari on paraffin. In the belief that a sound manufacturing base is important for any country, this book therefore looks at how to effectively implement and use MRP/MRPII systems to ensure that manufacturing survives in all countries wise enough to understand its importance.

I have it on good authority that techniques akin to MPS and MRP (at least at a gross level) were used in aircraft factories during World War 1. I have been unable personally to verify this but it makes sense to me. The use of munitions and weapons in that conflict could not be drawn as a straight line on a graph. Although Hollywood would sometimes have us think otherwise, the land war (at least) of 1914-1918 was not 365 days a year of extreme activity. War was a series of 'pushes', each of which required months of planning and preparation. Each 'push' began with a bombardment, when thousands of guns fired millions of shells over a period of, typically, a week—an enormous spike on anyone's graph. At the same time, water cooled heavy machine guns were each firing up to 100,000 bullets in a twelve hour period, and air activity would also have peaked. That air activity would have called for reserves to have been built up, sufficient to cope with the heavy losses that could be expected.

What better way to cope with fluctuating heavy demand on factories with relatively constant output than Master Production Scheduling? Although not documented (at least not anywhere that is accessible to me), it is reasonable to assume that, having produced a production plan that facilitated a stock build-up for the beginning of the 'push' (something, incidentally, that reorder point control (ROP) could not have coped with), someone would have multiplied the parts list (rudimentary bill of material) by those numbers to produce time-phased demand on the suppliers of engines, wheels, instruments and everything else that went into the final aircraft.

It is, by the way, interesting to note that the aero engines companies of Rolls Royce and General Electric were, amongst others, leaders in computerised MRP in the early 1950s, having used manual versions for many years prior to that. I wonder where and when those good habits were born: perhaps they didn't forget the lessons of 1914–1918 and consequently didn't go back to 'tried and tested' methodologies in 1919.

Incidentally, I was amused, when speaking to a Rolls Royce old-timer some years ago, to find out what drove RR to computerise their MRP system. It wasn't, as I thought, as simple as just wanting to be more efficient. As with most successful system implementations, there was a real driver, a real need. In those early post-WWII years, there was still heavy demand for their output, as the world re-armed in the hope of deterring the next conflict. Consequently a build programme was agreed by the Board of Directors every month and released to the factory. Exploding this build plan (effectively an MPS) manually through MRP took 19 days and, in consequence, the plan changed about two days after the purchasing department reacted to it! RR realised that MRP was a good thing and realised that it had to improve the mechanics of it rather than abandon the logic of it. A sincere 'Thank you', Rolls Royce and General Electric.

After the pioneering work of RR and GE and the rest, other organisations got in on the act. For example, IBM introduced and sold a 'Bill of Materials Processor' (BOMP) from 1961 followed by the LAMP & PICS early MRP systems from the mid-60s. In the 70s, more sophisticated MRP & MRPII systems started to arrive (these were still the days of large mainframe computers, restricted to large and wealthy companies).

By the 1980s, rapidly falling computer hardware prices were matched by reducing software prices as more and more software companies (one could argue too many) got in on the act. By now, of course, MRP had evolved into MRPII as software companies responded to market demand and tried to add functionality to their offerings to out-do the competition.

At this stage, too, capacity schedulers began to appear. Initially horrendously expensive, a virtuous circle caused prices to drop as demand increased (I'll leave someone else to answer the chicken or egg question). MRPII systems had now matured and were seen as indispensable by class-leading manufacturing companies. They were also increasingly affordable and thus found their way into smaller and smaller companies (I have worked with companies of less than 20 people that are using MRPII successfully, intelligently and productively).

In the great rush to ERP, many MRPII systems were merely re-labelled although, in truth, many of the better ones had moved a long way in that direction before the term Enterprise Resource Planning had been coined. Even today, though, readers would be advised to check the functionality offered by particular ERP systems carefully and not just assume all such systems to be complete.

Year 2000 had good and bad effects on MRPII/ERP. In the panic to implement new systems, many companies made bad choices, the results of which are still being felt ten years on. Some companies were, frankly, taken for a ride by software companies who sold much more than they could deliver. The surge in growth in the systems market was such that software companies had to rapidly recruit and train consultants and not all of them did so successfully.

All of this resulted in scepticism, distrust and disillusionment which are preventing many companies from making the most of these systems even today. A "once bitten, twice shy" attitude is causing them now to under-invest in systems, training and consultancy. The damage may take years yet to repair.

One good outcome of Year2000, though, was that a lot of small software companies, which were barely viable and which never had sufficient resource to support their customers properly, went to the wall because they couldn't afford the costs of re-writing their software. The result is fewer but stronger system suppliers, more able to implement and support their systems properly. 'Caveat emptor' are still the by-words, though.

2. Why MRPII?

S ome things move in cycles in this world. No sooner has the case been made for company-wide integrated systems, with the move towards them seemingly inevitable and irreversible, than someone identifies a need for specialist systems at a departmental level. The result is that islands of information spring up again; each its own self-contained little universe, mindfully independent of, or ignorant of, other company systems. These departmental systems can rarely be part of a coherent whole for several reasons:

- In optimising them for their stated task, the wants and needs of other departments are necessarily ignored.
- Because optimisation is at departmental level, there will be no standardisation across departments. Most obviously, this will express itself in a disparity of databases, file structures, operating systems and sometimes even coding structures, such that, even if attempts are made to share information, it becomes very difficult to do so and to do so quickly and reliably.

Take for example a real-life manufacturing company that had three sets of stock figures: manufacturing, sales and warehousing each had their own stock control system and, you will not be surprised to hear, none of them agreed. Regardless of the technical challenges of sharing data between those three systems, even if it was attempted there would be the considerable challenge of getting people to agree which figures were right. Maintaining accurate stock figures in one system is hard enough but the problem worsens exponentially as the number of systems increases. (That the time and effort required to transact every movement three times is wasteful is hopefully self-evident.)

Stock control is just one facet of this problem, of course. If the stock figures don't agree, then probably the sales figures don't agree: nor the costing figures. What did we make last week? We can't agree. What did we sell last week? We can't agree. What were our cost of sales figures? Given the responses to the previous questions: almost certainly inaccurate. Will we still be in business next year? Do we deserve to be?

The truth is that you cannot optimise the bottom line by optimising independently each of the elements that contribute to it. All elements must co-exist seamlessly. If my business is making motor vehicles, it is not much good having the world's best and most efficient one litre engine when the rest of the factory are building 10-ton trucks. Manufacturing today, more than ever, has to be a team game: we can't all be the star player and we definitely can't each have our own ball.

The essence of an MRPII system is that it takes demand and, through MRP, generates both purchasing and manufacturing recommendations and then sees these through to fulfilment. At the front end comes forecast or actual demand and at the back end comes customer payments. In the middle comes everything that is required to turn plans into reality, to monitor and adjust those plans and to analyse the results. None of this is easy and it is impossible to be around such systems for long without hearing tales of woe from people who have experienced, and have been scarred by, failed attempts at their implementation.

Bad experiences cause people to withdraw to environments that they feel comfortable in. They will be drawn to the tried and tested, even though they know these to be less than ideal. Better a horse and cart that works, they feel, than a sports car that doesn't. That's fine; at least until your competitors get their sports cars running.

But what is the 'tried and tested'? In the immediate post-war years, probably through to the mid-60s, there was a shortage of manufactured goods at a time when living standards were rising and people had money that was burning holes in their pockets. In those circumstances, companies didn't worry about efficiency or quality—they focused on quantity; getting the maximum quantity of product out of the door (even today, such attitudes live on; although increasingly rarely as the companies where they survive do not).

These were also times when innovation was not the king that it is today. Companies could, and did, survive by making the same old thing in the same old way. Readers of a certain age will remember when the British car industry produced cars in which heaters were optional extras and when the British motorcycle industry produced bikes that required kick-starting. They made a lot of money until one day the Japanese started doing things differently. British ways were 'tried and tested' but, what consolation that was to the millions who subsequently joined the dole queues, I will leave the reader to decide.

What 'tried and tested' methodology did these manufacturers retreat to? First and foremost was Reorder Point (ROP) backed up by Economic Order Quantity (EOQ). Remind me later to also to also talk to you about Contract MRP; another dinosaur that refused to lie down.

However; back to ROP. The great attraction of ROP and EOQ is that, though severely limited in their effectiveness, they are easy: easy to implement and easy to run. The fact that they can therefore be run by comparatively unqualified (i.e. cheap) staff was probably not lost on companies that thought that keeping costs down was an infallible route to improving profits.

To understand the attractiveness of ROP and EOQ, beyond the fact that they are cheap, let's look again at the environment that spawned them. For the first few hundred years of industrialisation, design changes were only tolerated if substantial advantage was to accrue. This was not just conservatism but a reflection of the fact that change was expensive and disruptive: production would inevitably fall during the change-over period.

For good examples of this, consider the manufacture of aircraft and tanks during the Second World War. Britain found herself continuing the production of obsolescent equipment because it was thought better to have a continuing supply of second rate weapons than to risk shortages whilst production lines were turned over to the manufacture of first rate replacements. The Battle, the Whitley and the Blenheim should never have been frontline aircraft for as long as they were.

The problems with tank manufacture were, if anything, even greater. Tanks need complex and expensive jigs for their manufacture. In those days, such jigs took between one and two years to manufacture and get right. In retrospect it seems incredible but, in 1940, the British War Cabinet Committee ordered that tank production, and I quote, "must not be interfered with either by the incorporation of improvements to the approved types or by the production of newer models".

Before you take this as a criticism of Britain and British attitudes only, remember that the Ford Model 'T' was in production from 1908 until 1927 (and the Ford Popular of the mid-50s would have been recognisable to a car mechanic of the mid-30s). From the car industry, throw in also the Renault 2CV and the Austin Ambassador: I'm sure that you can think of other examples. (If I appear to be unfairly picking on the motor industry, let me admit that my first job in industry was with a tier 2 supplier.)

Going back to military analogies; around the world, navies clung to sail, armies clung to cavalry and air forces clung to biplanes. Sometimes it was costs, sometimes it was 'better the devil you know' but perhaps too often it was an unwillingness to try something new lest it drag us out of our comfort zone. It is also worth remembering that, in the sixties, many members of middle and senior management would have been though WWII and must inevitably have carried from it experiences and attitudes that would have still been influencing their thinking even then. The desire to get as much as possible through the factory gates would have been close to overwhelming. Naively, more production meant more profit to those who had been brought up that way.

Continuing the production of 'tried and tested' products then made stock control easy. With a relatively small range of products in more or less constant production (and few design changes) stock control was merely a question of maintaining agreed stock levels rather than of doing anything clever (don't forget that, in a market that has money to spend and is starved of products, efficiency and cost control are not as important as achieving high output). And don't forget also that, whilst MRPII systems require trained and qualified staff to operate them, a ROP inventory control system can be operated by a low-level storeman: management in those days perhaps understood saving money better than they understood making money.

So stock control was a stores function whilst frequently purchasing was either a finance department function or a function under very tight senior management control (typically a storeman would write out a requisition for senior management approval and this would subsequently be turned into a purchase order by a clerk). An attempt was made to apply a 'scientific' approach by calculating 'Economic Order Quantities" (EOQ). I guess that, in the absence of anything better, ROP and EOQ were better than nothing but it is a fine call.

So what is wrong with ROP, given that it is cheap to implement and cheap to run? In conversation with an old-timer a number of years back, he likened running a system on ROP to driving your car by looking in the rear view mirror: if the future is the same as the past, you won't have a problem.

ROP is rearward looking and reactive. In environments where demand for the end product is relatively stable (when making Model 'T' Fords, to establish a production plan, you merely asked yourself how many you could produce: that was your production plan) you can assume that demand for components is also stable.

Don't forget that we are looking at an era when designs didn't change much and when options and choices were severely limited. When Henry Ford gave the customer just one choice of colour, he was focused on efficiency but he definitely also made life easier for whoever it was who looked after the stock control of paint! Design changes (remember the tanks) would have been few and far between, giving ample time for new reorder points and EOQs to be calculated, even if this was necessary. Frequently it wouldn't have been, as there were so few models offered that it would have been just a case for replacing blue widgets on the line by red widgets—if I am replacing the Mark 1 component by the Mark 2, potential output of the finished product would have been unlikely to change markedly, if at all. All I need to worry about, as a stock controller, is running down my safety stocks (or transferring them to the spares department) as the new widget is introduced. Then it's back to measuring stock against ROP and raising requisitions when I seem to be getting low.

Again, lest we forget, the big crime at the time was running out of stock; not having too much of it. JIT hadn't been invented and would, indeed, probably have been unwelcome, as low stock levels would have been considered a danger to the Holy Grail of maximising production quantity. Stock represented continuity and, if things went pear-shaped, flexibility. (And our financial people said that it was an asset!)

ROP, being rearward looking, doesn't cope well with irregular demand and absolutely hates supersessions and design changes. As a final warning, let me throw in a story about a 'buy and sell' organisation that I know. They buy and sell household items and have buyers across the world looking for deals. These buyers have considerable freedom as they rarely get things wrong. But sometimes they do.

One buyer bought a 40 foot container load of a product that just didn't sell and which sat at the back of the warehouse for, and I'm not exaggerating, years. Eventually the company told its salespeople to take whatever they could for them, just to get rid of them. No price was to be too low as long as the warehouse got cleared. They told all of the sales people but no-one thought to tell the stock controller. Shortly after, he looked at his stock reports and saw that, not only were these things now flying out of stock, he was in danger of running out of them. Yes, you guessed it; he hit ROP and ordered another container load.

A further failing of ROP systems is that they give the shop floor no idea of priorities. When ROP is hit, a replenishment order is immediately suggested whether or not the items are required in the short term. Whilst this is not too bad for items in daily use, it is wasteful for items that have sporadic or lumpy demand. Resources (capacity and materials) are then consumed when there could be higher priorities: at best, there could be a log-jam in the factory caused by the release of un-necessary orders. The jobs that were really needed could be 'lost' (sometimes literally) in a sea of WIP.

Enter the Progress Chasers (or Expeditors, as they were also sometimes called). Telling their story will demonstrate just how far production planning and control has come in the leading companies since MRP/ MRPII first took off. For the benefit of readers who did not study ancient history at school (and with apologies to companies that still employ, if not such job titles, such techniques) let me explain the function of such individuals.

In days when production planning was as described previously (i.e. merely giving the factory Works Orders / Job Cards, call them what you will), there was no proper planning and therefore no control of what went on on the shop floor. Individual departmental foremen were given jobs to do and then expected to just get on with it. There were no systems that told people where jobs were, what progress had been made on them, and which was required next. There would, of course, have been some sort of date, or dates, on the works orders but no-one would have given these much notice as they would more often than not have specified a date in the past.

At this point, you are saying to yourself (I hope), "That is crazy!" And you would be right. So let me explain what went on in those days and how this crazy situation came about.

Firstly, when receiving a new order from a customer, few companies had systems to tell them how much work they already had on their books. Calculating a delivery date was, at best, guesswork and frequently wasn't done at all: in these circumstances, the delivery date was frequently the customer's requested delivery date! (A typical quote from a sales person in those days would have been, "If we had quoted the customer a reasonable delivery date, we wouldn't have got the order.").

No-one took production planning seriously because, as mentioned before, companies saw their objective as getting as much out the door as possible and, if this meant ignoring delivery promises, then this was seen as a small price to pay. So works orders were released to the shop floor with totally unrealistic due dates. When confronted by meaningless dates, foremen could only assume that the jobs with the earliest dates were the ones that were required first.

Reasonable as this sounds, don't forget that the due date was frequently the customer's required date. This would not matter if the factory had sufficient capacity to give all customers all that they wanted, when they wanted it but this would have required massive excess capacity to cope with spiky demand so the inevitable result (doubtless aided and abetted by over-promising) was that jobs, in at least the customer's eyes, became late. And some of these customers would have been recognised as being important.

When the customer complained, as inevitably they did, something would have to be done. The norm then was that the factory would be informed that particular orders were to given priority to get them through production and out to the customer. But, without proper systems, how was that to be managed?

In those days, most manufacturing companies had at least one progress chaser (a Progress Department was not unknown). His job (I'm not being sexist here: Progress Chasers were invariably male) was first to go onto the shop floor to find where the job was. He would then identify which stage of manufacture it had reached and physically move it to the area or machine where it needed to be next; verbally telling the operator or foreman that this was to be the next job to be processed and, for good measure, possibly annotating the paperwork to show that this was a priority job in the, generally vain, hope that this would expedite its flow subsequently. (For particularly important jobs, existing jobs would be stopped to allow the priority job to be processed immediately.) The progress chaser would then keep his eye on the job, nudging it through the manufacturing process until it finally was despatched. All of this doesn't sound so unreasonable, so what could and did go wrong?

Well; in those days, it was not unusual to have large numbers of late orders. As late as the eighties, I joined a company in which over 90% (yes, you heard that right; 90%) of customer orders were overdue. In those circumstances, there was not just one priority job at most work centres: there were many. Conflict was inevitable as multiple jobs competed for finite resource: a situation that could be exacerbated when a company had more than one progress chaser.

I remember well how we addressed this problem of priorities when I was in my first job in manufacturing. Foremen were, not unreasonably, pointing out that, if everything was urgent, then nothing was urgent. They asked for jobs to be prioritised. Our progress chaser quickly came up with the answer: priority jobs would be marked with a red star. Brilliant!

The problem was that, after a few weeks, most jobs were marked with a red star. Never mind: really urgent jobs would get two stars! Brilliant! A few weeks later and really, really, really urgent jobs were being marked with four stars. We gave up.

Well; we didn't actually give up. We went back to the sales people and asked them to prioritise. The answer came back: ("Everything is a priority and, if you can't cope, that's not our fault."!) We then came up with a novel concept—Production Planning! We decided our own priorities—big customers first. Their jobs got scheduled first through all departments, one job at a time, and the small customers got whatever capacity was left. We upset a lot of people but we had a plan! And we started to give realistic delivery promises on new orders. The fact that these were generally not passed on by our Sales Department ("If we tell the customer the truth, we won't get the order!") did not invalidate what we did; just lessened the value of it to the company.

Having made a plan, we stuck to our guns, saying that we now had a something that we believed in. Nothing could be added to the plan; nothing could be pushed in or moved forward, unless something was taken out to make room for it. If this was a novel, this story would have a happy ending. But it isn't, and it doesn't. Our sales people continued to tell the customer what they thought the customer wanted to hear, rather than the truth. We, as a company, had not all learned that manufacturing was a team game.

As a company, we probably survived initially because our competition was as bad as we were but that can never be a strategy for long-term survival. Inevitably, some other companies got themselves sorted out and their market share increased as a result. To allow the good companies to increase market share, the second-raters got squeezed out. The company folded.

When Production can't make all that Sales can sell, is it the fault of Production or is it the fault of Sales for selling too much? Perhaps they are selling too cheaply? Or is it the fault of Design for creating products which require too much time and resource to produce? Or can we blame someone (anyone) else? No: to survive, we need more than just someone to blame: all departments must make a positive contribution, regardless of whose 'fault' it is.

In comparison with ROP/EOQ, MRPII is forward looking. Demand is, or should be, driven only by actual sales orders or by forecasts that someone has signed off. Sometimes those forecasts have to be at sub-assembly or raw material level (and we'll look at that also later) but the key is that the humans in the loop are not merely functionaries, blindly reacting to triggers. They are, or should be, well-paid and well-educated professionals, capable of making the company a lot of money by using their brains in a structured and disciplined environment. Someone older and wiser that I (well; wiser anyway) once said that MRPII is not a computer system, but a people system that just happens to run on a computer.

MRP/MRPII, then, can cope with change. Spikey demand does not spike its guns. Moreover, it can cope with the proliferation of variants, options and design changes that from the sixties onwards became the norm in an increasing number of industries. Henry Ford must be spinning like a top in his grave.

3. How does it work?

This has been written as a standalone chapter so that, if you already have a good understanding of MRP and MRPII you can by-pass it. It might be worth a quick scan even if you are already expert, though, as you might find things to disagree with!

In essence, MRP takes demand and turns it into supply recommendations. Elements of MRPII, such as purchase order processing and works order processing, then take these recommendations and facilitate them, whilst a plethora of other elements such as capacity planning & scheduling, WIP tracking, costing etc do their part also.

Let's first look at the building blocks of MRPII before we consider how they all fit together. In this book, I will try to use standard terminology. But, whatever the text books say, terminology will often differ as we move from country to country and even from company to company. Frequently, new terms are coined by MRPII/ ERP software suppliers that are keen to differentiate their system from their competitors' offerings. For this reason, you may find me defining words and terms apparently unnecessarily. Please bear with me: if there is a chance of my being misunderstood, I would rather be accused of being pedantic than being wrong.

3.1 Master Production Scheduling

Firstly, the Master Production Schedule (MPS). Earlier generations would have called this the production plan but cynics would say that it is easier to sell expensive consultancy on Master Production Scheduling than it is on production planning. They probably have a point: I remember the days when company directors thought that production planning was a clerical function that involved no more than creating Works Orders and sorting them by one criteria or another before passing them to the factory.

Early proponents of MRPII, such as Plossl, Orlicky and Wight, saw production planning and control as much more than a clerical activity. It was to be carried out by trained and qualified professionals and had a critical importance to the wellbeing of the company that used it. Production planning and control was to be more than just pushing work into the factory through one door and, with the aid of 'progress chasers', pulling it out of the other.

Most text books say that Master Production Scheduling is essential to a manufacturing company's survival but I think that is too general a statement. If you are a MTS (Make-to-stock) or ATO (Assemble-to-order) company, then I would agree but, if you are a MTO (Make-to-order) company, I would like to debate this apparent truism. But first let's justify Master Production Scheduling in MTS and ATO companies.

If you have always have capacity greater than you need (which would be unusual) or if you can easily turn on overtime or extra shifts (which can be expensive), then you don't have a problem as your order book (or sales forecast) can be your MPS. More likely, you have spikey demand or bottlenecks in your production processes. The production plan (MPS) must be realistic and achievable: it should not (with the exception of the unusual circumstances above) be raw customer requirements, pushed into a mincing machine in the hope that what comes out is good enough. Something that is frequently ignored is that, in MTS companies in particular, the MPS must also support the company's business objectives and this is where what used to be called 'Closed loop MRP' comes in. We will discuss that shortly but first I want to debate MPS in an MTO company. We will return to looking at how to create an MPS later.

3.2 MPS in a Make to Order Company

We have already said that the purpose of a MPS is to create a production plan that can be agreed by:

- Production as being achievable
- Sales as being the best fit to their requirements as can be achieved in an imperfect world
- Finance as providing a manageable cash flow and giving a reasonable return on investment.

So why would the rules in a Make to Order company be different? Well; the whole point of an MPS is that it is something that can be changed, adjusted and amended until we are happy with it. Quantities can be changed and requirement dates can be changed until we achieve the best possible fit.

Compare that to the situation at a Make to Order company. There, we start with two assumptions:

- That the order will be delivered on-time against the promised delivery, and
- That the full quantity will be delivered.

If we can't meet these criteria, then the terms of the order should have been re-negotiated before we accepted it. So we have to start with an assumption that we will keep our promises (certainly if we want to be sure of repeat business). That means that we can't copy our order book into the MPS and start to adjust it there. If we aim to be a professional organisation with a good future, we should be building systems that help us keep our promises, not make it easy and routine to break them.

Having set that rule, I would allow two exceptions to it:

1. If we have spikey demand, I would recognise the need for jobs to be pulled **forward** to smooth production.
2. If we are a mix of MTO & MTS, then a viable way of coming up with a good production plan would be to drop both sets of requirements into an MPS so that the MTS element can be adjusted around a fixed MTO schedule.

3.3 MPS—At what level of the bill of material?

It is generally assumed that master production scheduling should be carried out at the end-item, or SKU, level and frequently this is the correct thing to do: but not always. Consider the following four kinds of company:

- Company A is the classic MRP company, as represented by Rolls Royce and General Electric. This type of company has a relatively small number of end items (SKUs) but a large number of purchased items.
- Company B is quite the opposite; having a small number of raw materials but a large number of end items. Examples of this type of company are frequently found in the plastics industries.
- Company C is a company that builds a relatively small number of common sub-assemblies from a fair number of raw materials and then produces a large number of variants of their products using these sub-assemblies. They are usually configure-to-order (CTO) companies and PC manufacture would be a good example.
- Company D has a relatively small number of raw materials that get turned into many components and sub-assemblies that are then turned into a small number of end products. A manufacturer of wooden garden buildings would fall into this category.

The essence of master production scheduling is that it is carried out by production planners (i.e. people) and demand for sub-assemblies and components (dependant demand) is calculated by MRP. Not surprisingly, given that MRP & MPS came originally from type A companies, they work very well there.

Consider, though, type B companies which can have a very large number of SKUs. Manual scheduling now becomes very much harder because there are simply so many products to consider. On the other hand, in these kinds of company, complex bills of material are not the norm and manufacturing lead times are generally short, so it is raw material supply that is the key. If you plan your materials well (see forecasting and The Law of Big Numbers), you have a good chance of making anything you need (assuming that you have sufficient capacity).

Type C companies need to concentrate on their sub-assemblies as, if they get these right, configuring the final items is relatively straight forward. They can also use The Law of Big Numbers to decide how many of these they should be making: I worked with a PC manufacturer who was using an MRPII system to offer next-day despatch on all sales orders. This, incidentally, worked because the bulk of the combined manufacture and purchase lead time, if you look again at the diagram, is always below the narrowest point. Type A companies tend to have long lead times for both manufactured and purchased items, type B companies tend to have short manufacturing lead times, type C companies will have short manufacturing lead times for the configuration element of their manufacture and type D companies are very similar to type A. Incidentally; this narrow point is often a good place to hold safety stock.

Type D companies, as we said, are very similar to type A companies but with simpler raw material requirements.

By concentrating manual planning on these narrowest points, we are dealing with the least possible number of parts and the task becomes much more manageable.

3.4 Closed Loop MRP

By way of introduction to this chapter, I have to admit to a little game that I play sometimes when I meet senior management of a new client. When I am in a mischievous mood, I am wont to ask them why their company exists. Sadly, even from senior management in large companies, I frequently get the answer I expect rather than the answer that I want. The answer will too often be along the lines of "We are here to make furniture / electrical goods / pharmaceuticals" or whatever. Occasionally they will try to quote some trite company mission statement: "We are here to service the needs of the widget industry" or some such banality.

Wrong! Your company is here to make money! Only by doing so can it survive. You can make the best widgets imaginable, you can be recognised industry-wide for your quality, you can excel at 'investing in your people' but if you don't make money you might as well close up and go home now. Your company has no future.

One of the big challenges for manufacturing companies in making money is spikey demand. Both make-to-order and make-to-stock companies have the perpetual problem of customers not ordering what they want them to order, when they want them to order it. Sometimes these companies contribute to their own problem by offering customers discounts based on individual order quantities and not yearly totals. The result is that demand comes in big chunks, rather than a regular flow, and they can do little more than hope that things even out across their customer base.

There is also frequently the problem of seasonality in order intake. We can all understand why this should be the case in the ice cream industry or the Christmas card industry but it occurs in more industries than we might at first imagine, from pet food to car parts (animals eat more in cold weather, less in hot and new car sales (in the UK at least) are influenced by the new registration numbers and this means that servicing, and subsequently repairs, are unevenly spread over the year).

On the grounds that a picture speaks a thousand words, the following diagram will help.

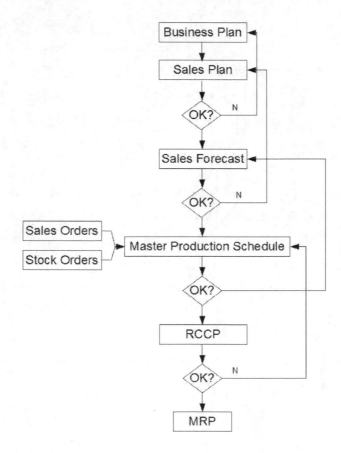

To begin with, the company has an overall objective—to make money. It must ask itself how much money it needs to make to justify the investment that has been made in its creation. If I have spent five million pounds in setting up a company, am I happy to make one thousand pounds per year profit? Clearly not: I would be much better off leaving the money in the bank. So I must have a clear idea of how much profit I want to make every year. I must have a business plan which, at its simplest, might say that I intend to make one million pounds a year profit by making and selling widgets.

I must then plan (there's that word again!) how to make that profit. If I make widgets, I need to decide how many I can sell, and at what price. I must have a reasonable idea of my costs, even if I am in a volatile market place where material costs are not stable. I need to know, even if I can't know exactly, how much profit I am likely to make on each widget that I sell. If that expected profit per widget multiplied by the number of widgets that I expect to sell doesn't give me the profit that I need, then there is no point going on.

I have to loop back to the previous stage; my business plan. If I can't sell enough widgets at a price that generates the profit I need, then I have to rethink my plan. Can I settle for a reduced profit and still justify the company's existence? Do I need to make other products as well as, or instead of, widgets? I need to go round and round that loop until I have a sales plan that makes sense and looks as if it will give me the profit I need (hence 'closed loop').

I then need to create a sales forecast. It's not enough to say that my plan is to sell a quantity of widgets: what specifically am I going to sell, to whom and when? (We will look at forecasting and 'The Law of Big Numbers' later.) The sales plan must be viable and not just a wish list—is there a market for what I plan to sell?

The next stage is to create a Master Production Schedule (MPS) to test whether I can actually make what I expect to sell. If I can't make enough widgets to satisfy my sales plan, I again have to loop back a stage. Can I change my sales plan? Can I sell different widgets at different prices? If so, I can change my sales plan and move on to the MPS stage again.

If not, I have to loop back again to the business plan stage. I now know that I can't make the necessary profit by making and selling my million widgets. So I have to change my business plan. Should I look at expanding my production facility? Should I consider sub-contracting some production? Should I move out of the widget business?

These are business level decisions and decisions that have to be made if my plans are to be anything more than a pair of crossed fingers. At each stage, the plan has to be tested and, if it doesn't work, I have to loop back and rethink the previous stage. The key thing is that, however many iterations it takes, the end result has to be a viable and achievable plan that is agreed by Production, Sales and Finance. Only that will give the required overall result: that of achieving the business plan. Anything less is a failure and, if not corrected, will result in the demise of the company.

The 'looping' process described above has now been given the name "Sales and Operations Planning". I don't plan to go into great detail on it here, as sufficient good books have been published on it already. Suffice to say that it involves functional managers of the above named departments sitting down together, setting aside 'point scoring' tendencies, and agreeing what should be made and when. That involves team work, compromises and professional attitudes: it's not about individual departments winning and losing, it's about doing what is best for the company. It requires maturity on the part of all participants: if you don't think that your management team is up to it, consider pulling in an external mentor to sit-in on meetings until all the pennies have dropped.

But how does MRP itself work? Again, a picture will speak a thousand words.

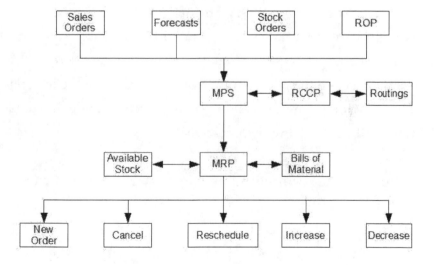

The purpose of MRP is to balance supply with demand. As mentioned before, it has been around for quite a time so it is quite good at it and, when it goes wrong, it is almost always the case that it has been set up incorrectly or that the data is wrong. The logic works.

Demand can come from several sources; most frequently the following:

- Actual sales orders from customers
- Forecast sales orders from customers
- A make-to-stock requirement
- Re-order points (ROP)

Generally, systems allow actual sales orders to be netted off against forecasts so that demand is not duplicated. In real life, when a forecast doesn't firm up, there will be a point when we want to ignore the unconsumed part of it. One very obvious reason is production lead times: if it takes two weeks to make something, when we get towards the end of the month we will simply run out of time and the order will have to go into the next month. Note that when we process sales forecasts in MRP, we are forecasting when the products are due to be delivered and not when we expect to receive the order.

Having gathered the demand, we want to make sure, before we order all necessary materials, that we can actually make those items. We can do this by dropping the demand into a Master Production Schedule (MPS) and running a capacity planning tool such as Rough Cut Capacity Planning against this. Later on, we will discuss the level in the bill of material that we should be creating the MPS at but, at this stage, we will assume that we are scheduling at the top (SKU) level, as this is most common.

In simpler environments, it is possible to drop raw demand (orders, forecasts etc) directly into the capacity planner and avoid the MPS. The MPS allows production dates and quantities to be amended easily but, in a make-to-order (MTO) environment, this is frequently not acceptable for received orders, so all that can be moved or amended are any requirements that have been driven by ROP or where requirement quantities have been inflated by a minimum batch size. In an MTO environment, if we cannot adjust capacity by turning on overtime, extra shifts or sub-contracting, we should run a capacity check before confirming a delivery date with the customer. Customers do not like broken delivery promises—ask your buyers!

Having satisfied ourselves that we have sufficient capacity available, we can run the demand though MRP (Materials Requirements Planning) which will work its way down the bill of material step by step, using the same logic all the time. The following diagram illustrates this logic.

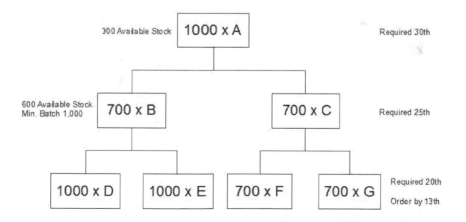

In this simple example, we will assume a seven day working week, a five day manufacturing lead time for manufactured items and a ten day purchasing lead time for all purchased items. We will also assume required quantities of one for every sub-assembly and item. Real life is rarely that symmetrical but it is the logic that is important to us here and not the numbers. We will also set a minimum batch size of 1,000 on the assembly B to see the effect of that.

1. There is a demand for 1,000 of Product A on the 30th of the month, but MRP recognises a free stock of 300 (there may also be an overage being made on an existing works order if Product A has a minimum batch size and we will call this mix of free stock and due-in spare stock, available stock.) MRP netts off the 300 against the 1,000 and calculates that we need to make only 700. Demand for 700 sets of sub-assemblies is then passed down to the next level. Because Product A has a 5-day lead time, the sub-assemblies must be ready by the 25th.

2. MRP checks the Bill of Material (BoM) and calculates that 700 of sub-assembly B and 700 of sub-assembly C are required. It again checks for available stock and finds that we have 600 Bs spare, so the nett requirement for that item is 100. However, we have a minimum batch size of 1,000 on this sub-assembly so the required quantity is increased to that number. There is no available stock of sub-assembly, and no minimum batch size, for sub-assembly C so that requirement stays at 700. Demand for materials for 1000 of sub-assembly B and 700 of sub-assembly C is passed down to the next level. With a 5-day manufacturing lead time for the sub-assemblies B and C, the components required for them must be available by the 20th.

3. MRP checks the BoM for sub-assembly B and finds that 1,000 of component D and 1,000 of component E are required. Likewise a demand for 700 each of components F and G is calculated. MRP again checks for available stock of these and calculates a nett quantity to order although, as these are purchased items, the requirements are not exploded further. At this level, the requirements are very frequently automatically adjusted to take into account minimum order quantities and pack sizes. As these components have a 7–day purchasing lead time, they must be ordered by the 13th.

In the above example, items are scheduled to be available on the day that they are wanted. Systems are frequently configured so that they are available the day before, so that they can be booked into stock and moved to where they are required.

3.5 Capacity Planning and Scheduling

Key to testing the viability of the MPS is knowing whether or not we have, or will have, sufficient manufacturing capacity to meet it. I make a clear differentiation between capacity planning and capacity scheduling. To me, capacity planning is deciding how much capacity I need so that I can ensure that I have it when I need it. Turning on extra capacity cannot always been done quickly as it can mean the construction of new facilities and the purchase of new plant; not just recruiting extra staff. I may have to look at capacity requirements far beyond my current order book and this will rely on a realistic forecast of future sales.

Because capacity planning is a medium to long term tool (capacity shortages have to be identified sufficiently far out in the future to allow remedial action to be taken), it cannot be 100% accurate and any time taken to try to make it so is wasted. It will generally be looking at sales forecasts, which themselves can rarely approach 100%, so having a tool that works quickly and allows multiple iterations is more useful than a tool that promises a meaningless accuracy.

Capacity scheduling, on the other hand, is a shorter-range tool that allows us to get the most that we can from our pint pot: i.e. to optimise existing capacity. Inevitably the two over-lap. In Planning, we must start with looking at what can be achieved with existing capacity before modelling new resources, whilst modern capacity scheduling tools will give us a 'what if?' capability to decide whether, for example, overtime will solve the problem, at least in the short term.

Capacity scheduling is a much more complex beast than capacity scheduling and many companies struggle to justify the extra cost so a detailed look at how both work, and what they can and cannot do, may be helpful.

3.5.1 Capacity Planning

This is sometimes called Infinite Capacity Planning or Rough Cut Capacity Planning (RCCP for short).

As mentioned above, this is a medium to long-term tool to help ensure that the Master Production Schedule is viable and to give advance notice of when additional capacity needs to be turned on;

either permanently through the introduction of additional plant, or temporarily through the addition of overtime or extra shifts. It is not the job of Capacity Planning to sequence or optimise jobs in production (that is the task of Capacity Scheduling) and so we are not looking for finite accuracy. Capacity Planning will frequently run in weekly time buckets, as opposed to the hours and minutes of Capacity Scheduling. Its job is to identify if and when extra resource is required and, at that level, hours and minutes are meaningless when the results are displayed.

The base data, on the other hand, does have to get down to hours and minutes so that the results are sensible. RCCP will be asked to check that sufficient capacity is available to meet the medium to long term plan. To do that, it has to multiply the amount of work to be done by the amount of time that is required to do that work. Let's say that our MPS calls for 1000 Type One widgets to be made in the first week in January. Our routing might say that, to make a widget, I need one hour in the machine shop, one quarter of an hour in the paint shop and a quarter of an hour in the packing area. Multiplying that out, I need:

- 1000 hours in the machine shop,
- 250 hours in the paint shop, and
- 250 hours in packing

to make Type One widgets in the first week of January (note that it doesn't matter which day, or days, in that week that the widgets will be made on. Apart from anything else, I am probably running this plan out so far in the future that any such accuracy would be spurious. Some RCCP systems, though, do recognise that operations at the beginning of the manufacturing process will, at least in the case of long production lead-time items, take place in earlier weeks than final assembly and packing, and these may produce more-accurate results in some companies.)

RCCP will then calculate the time requirements for all of the other things that I plan to make and the result will be a report that shows whether the plan has generated a realistic demand on factory resource. Frequently, capacity utilisation will also be displayed as a percentage of availability so that resources that are critically loaded can be quickly identified.

If there is insufficient manufacturing resource to meet the plan, there are only two alternatives:

- Increase the resource available, by adding extra shifts or plant, or by sub-contracting.
- Change the plan.

Continuing with fingers crossed, hoping that 'something will happen', is not an intelligent option.

For RCCP to work you need an accurate picture of what you want to produce and an accurate picture of how long it takes to produce those items. This latter requirement may not be as easy to satisfy as it sounds, for three reasons:

- Many companies, with the death of time & motion study, do not have accurate information on how long it takes to make their products. There may have been timings created for costing or for bonus purposes but are they really accurate? Frequently the former reflect assumptions and the latter reflect what the operators want management to believe! The first task, when introducing RCCP is therefore to get good, reliable timings. If you can't do that, it probably isn't worth continuing. The best you will be able to do, using flawed or inaccurate timings, is to ascertain that a department or machine is producing, say, 1200 hours' worth of output per week (regardless of the actual hours worked) and use that as the capacity norm, but such a crude approach will fail if the timing inaccuracies are not uniform across the product range.

Even when you get to a stage of knowing how long it takes to process each widget, in most industries you will have to make allowances for rejects and rework. It is not always possible to predict these with accuracy, as the problem may be caused by a number of things, including unpredictable processes and varying raw material quality. Nonetheless it is important that you factor these variables into the plan. If we have, on average, to make 1050 items to get the 1000 good ones that we need through inspection, then the plan needs to recognise this.

- The second problem that you have to overcome, assuming that you have accurate timings and can avoid going the crude route as described above, is to know how many hours per week usable capacity you actually have. A particular machine might nominally run 8 hours a day, five days a week. So available capacity is 40 hours per week: right?

  Wrong: I have never seen a machine (or person) produce at 100% of its theoretical output rate. There will be breakdowns, interruptions and all manner of unplanned events. When assessing capacity availability, we do ourselves no favours in assuming that things won't go wrong: we know that they will. There is no point, then, in measuring requirements against theoretical capacity. We need to compare against what I will call 'demonstrated capacity'. Analysis of past performance will tell us how many hours a day a machine or person actively produces. Frequently, in real life, I have found this to be about 85%: if you haven't calculated an actual figure for a department or machine (and the actual figure for different resources can well differ) it's not a bad place to start—that is 34 usable (demonstrated) hours out of a theoretical capacity of 40. Having done this, some of you will be tempted, when under pressure, to let the figure creep up again.

I understand this: it's hard to tell people that things can't be done because there is insufficient capacity when computer reports appear to show that six hours per week is going spare. But the point that we have to make sure that everyone understands is that we are loading against demonstrated capacity, not theoretical capacity. If your sales people insist that you load jobs against theoretical capacity, ask them if they will be happy when, in a few months' time, you advise them that the order wasn't fulfilled actually but it was theoretically!

• Lastly, in many industries there are still significant changeover times between jobs. These changeover times may not be fixed—it is not unusual in, for example, the plastics and food industries for changeover times to be product dependent. It takes longer to move from chocolate ice-cream to vanilla than it takes from vanilla to strawberry and it may not always be possible to model these changes far out unless there is a set cycle of changeovers.

Remember, RCCP is there to warn us when we don't have sufficient capacity. We can pretend we are OK, that we have sufficient capacity, that things will improve and we will be running at 90 or 95% demonstrated capacity by the time comes that we need it. But being professional also means facing up to bad news. If we have insufficient capacity, we need to do something about it. Merely hoping that things will improve, without doing something concrete to make them improve, is about as much use as sprinkling fairy dust in the factory.

We should also remember that, in most factories, it is unusual for there to be capacity problems in all work centres or on all machines. You might find that the 80/20 rule applies: that most of your problems are caused by a small number of resources. You probably recognise these already as being bottlenecks so you should focus your attention on these areas, particularly when it comes to calculating or measuring accurate process or run times. This will get you up and running faster and the reality is that we generally don't have to worry about that work stations that are significantly under-loaded.

Before we leave the topic of capacity planning; one last thought: we have been talking about capacity in terms of time but there can be other constraints. Space (whether for the assembly of large items or for the storage of stock built ahead of sales requirements) is sometimes an issue. Likewise, and particularly but not solely in the case of stock-build, do we have sufficient working capital? We will be procuring materials and maybe paying for them some time before we get paid by our customers for the finished items so we would be wise to ensure that our profitable business does not sink in the swamp of cash flow.

3.5.2 Capacity Scheduling

This is sometimes called Finite Capacity Planning or Finite Capacity Scheduling.

We have seen that Capacity Planning (RCCP) is a medium to long term tool. The short term is the prerogative of Capacity Scheduling. At this point, it is for most companies too late to solve capacity problems by installing extra plant or by recruiting extra staff (although short term overtime remains a possibility, albeit one that can incur an appreciable cost overhead). What is necessary now is to optimise the use of the capacity that we do have; to get as much as we can out of our pint pot.

To do this, we again need accurate detail of the tasks to be performed, the resource (people and/or plant) that will perform those tasks and the amount of time that is required to perform the tasks. Where capacity scheduling becomes more complex that capacity planning is in the options that now come into play. RCCP, being in time buckets of up to a week, would be happy to say that there was sufficient capacity in a five day week to both assemble and pack an item, but what if the assembly could not be completed until right at the end of the week? Packing capacity that was available earlier in the week (and satisfied RCCP) cannot be used (disappointingly, time only travels in one direction!). So capacity scheduling needs to consider, not only the time that operations take, but also their sequence.

Again; this may not be as easy as it sounds. Obviously we can't pack items until after they have been assembled but, in some manufacturing processes, operations can take place in parallel or in varying sequences. For example, if I am manufacturing wooden ladders, I might normally wait until the ladder is assembled before varnishing it but I could conceivably varnish the individual pieces before assembly if I had to. So in addition to ensuring that the data that capacity scheduling needs is accurate, we have to ensure that the 'rules' that we feed into it are not only accurate but complete. (If departmental foremen spot that they can improve the plan by, for example, swopping over the varnishing sequence mentioned above, they will do it if they feel it to be beneficial or easier. The planning system will then lose credibility and will soon be ignored.)

There are other things that we have to consider in the real world. Does one operation have to be completely finished before the next can begin or can operations overlap? For example, if I am assembling and packing one thousand widgets, do I have to wait for all one thousand to be assembled before packing can commence, or can packing begin after the first, say, one hundred have been completed? The rules will likely change from item to item and will have to consider factors like comparative run speeds of the two (or more) processes: i.e. packing could theoretically commence after one hundred widgets have been assembled but, because I can pack faster than I can assemble, I would soon 'catch up' and run out of packing work.

There is also, in many industries, the very significant factor of set-up times to consider. Although many companies for many years have been working hard to reduce machine set-up times, some things cannot be avoided. Going back to our ice cream analogy, I can change from vanilla to strawberry very quickly just by adding the strawberry concentrate and flushing though the first few litres as waste but, when I change from chocolate flavour back to vanilla, I have to do a complete clean-down of the machine. Similar problems occur in the plastics industry and doubtless others also.

The system must be set-up to 'understand' these factors; knowing that a perfect plan may be impossible. Minimising set-up times will increase throughput but it may do it at the expense of making some jobs late. Where is the balance to be? Obviously, if there is sufficient capacity for all requirements to be met on-time and with minimum set-up then we don't have a problem but life isn't always like that. Imagine that you did all the right things: you had an achievable MPS, you checked it against RCCP and the capacity schedule looked fine. Then real life kicked in. You had a machine breakdown, or a batch of faulty materials from a supplier that led to a higher than normal reject rate. The result is that you now have two or more jobs competing for priority at a particular resource.

I put this scenario to a client company that intended to implement a capacity scheduling system so that they could begin to formulate 'rules' for the system. "Easy!" they said, "The biggest customer gets priority." I then asked what they would want to happen if their three biggest customers were worth £7m, £6m and £5m respectively to them and the biggest customer had been given priority twice already this month at the expense of customers #2 and #3, who were now getting to be unhappy. What if giving the biggest customer (worth £7m) priority again was to cause the other two to walk? Individually they are worth less to the company than customer #1 but, collectively, we may be about to lose £11m worth of business to keep £7m. Do the rules now need to change?

I don't tell this tale because there is some magic formula that I am leading up to. I tell it to make you aware that implementing a capacity scheduling system (as, indeed, an ERP, MRPII or MRP system) is more than just loading data and pressing the switch. In this example, as in many others, there is no perfect answer. There are times when you just have to accept that individual people are going to be called upon to make human decisions and we need to build a system that not only recognises that but allows and facilitates it also.

Getting back to the basics, then; what we need for a capacity scheduling system to work are:

- Accurate data in our routings file
- A knowledge of when and how different operations can use alternative machines (e.g. can a job that is generally run on a CNC machine be transferred to a less-efficient lathe if shortage of capacity so dictates?)
- A knowledge of how set-up times can change according to job sequence (e.g. vanilla to strawberry ice cream and chocolate to vanilla)
- A knowledge of which operations can over-lap, and by how much
- Accurate data about machine capacities.

Let's revisit that last one again, even though we have already mentioned it already. How much work can be done in an eight hour shift? Eight hours' worth? No: we have already said that, allowing for all of the things that happen in real life, we may have to assume that only about 85% of time may be usable (remember the discussion on 'demonstrated capacity' versus theoretical capacity in section 3.5.1).

My favourite capacity scheduling systems recognise this and they allow entry of an efficiency factor against each resource. This says that, although a particular job may theoretically take an hour according to the data on the routing, a greater amount of time (say 70 minutes) may have to be allowed so that the 'Murphy factor' ("What can go wrong will go wrong") can be taken into account. Holding this efficiency factor as a percentage also allows new items of plant, which may take a while to settle down, to be planned initially at a reduced rate that then can be adjusted upwards as the new machine beds in (or downwards should age start to take its toll). If your chosen scheduling system does not offer such a facility, you may have to artificially truncate shifts so that, e.g., a 9-to-5 shift is established on the system as being only 9-to-4, so that the system will only load seven hours work to an eight hours shift.

There is one other complicating factor to consider when setting up your system. Let's assume that we have a resource that just works 9-to-5, Monday to Friday. If I am assembling one thousand widgets, it is probably not a problem if I can only assemble seven hundred by the end of Friday's shift and complete the last three hundred on Monday morning. However, if I am painting something, or baking something, that might not be possible. If I am baking one thousand cakes in a large oven, I can't 70% bake them on the Friday and 30% bake them on the Monday. In other words, I can't start a batch that I can't finish within the same shift. If you have similar scenarios you would be wise to check out how the scheduling systems that you are selecting from deal with these situations before you commit to them.

3.6 Bills of material

Generally, end items (SKUs or shippable items) are made from one or more levels of sub-assemblies which in turn are made from raw materials. Exceptions are industries where raw materials are turned into finished product in one process, but these are rare, as the finished product is usually packed after it has been produced and this may take place separately. For example, I may process olives to make olive oil but I will frequently put the oil into bulk tanks from where it will be packed off into differing sized containers subsequently.

Bills of material are sometimes (and wrongly) referred to as 'parts lists' but that is to do them a major disservice. In the olive oil example, my parts list would say that I need olives, bottles, labels and bottles. That is true but it gives me no idea of how things go together (imagine the parts list of a car).

If I am making a complete product in one process (using a single-level or 'flat' bill of material), this doesn't matter as I will want to have everything I need before I commence production. But, when making more-complex items, I may find that some items are not needed until well into the production process. For example, I might be making a large item over a period of days and not need the packaging items for it until I am ready to deliver it. In this instance, it is wasteful both in terms of money and of space to have the packaging available on day one.

So it is useful that my picture of how something goes together should have a time frame. Doing so will aid kitting when I come to draw parts and materials from the warehouse. It will also help me to time-phase the requirements so that, in long manufacturing lead-time situations, I am not tying up money and space unnecessarily early by bringing in materials before I actually need them.

An additional advantage of having bills of material is that, if a particular sub-assembly is used in the manufacture of a number of end products, I can call it up into those products as one item and not its list of constituent parts. (Imagine that you are a manufacturer of filing cabinets. The same design of drawer might be used in a range of cabinets. How much easier to have a bill of material for the drawer and call this up onto the bills for each cabinet that uses it, rather than to call up each of the components individually onto each new design.)

Clearly it is advantageous to have, rather than a crude parts list, a structured Bill of Material that shows how things go together and offers the possibility of time-phasing requirements for the components within it. Such a bill of material (BOM) would be called a multiple-level BOM, in which a finished item would be made up of sub-assemblies, each of which in turn might be made from sub-assemblies of their own (sub-sub-assemblies, if you like), all the way down to purchased items at the bottom.

3.7 Phantom bills of material

So what is a phantom bill of material (sometimes called a 'blow-through part') then? In the examples above, I have been assuming that one reason for having a structured BOM is that the sub-assemblies will likely be manufactured separately. In these circumstances, I probably want a separate works order for each sub-assembly (and another for the final assembly of all of the separate sub-assemblies into the finished article). But there were advantages to having a structured BOM which also hold true if manufacturing of my item is one continuous process.

Let's take as an example something as omnipresent as plastic waste bin liners. These will generally be made and packed in one continuous process. The manufacturing process would typically be something similar to the following:

- In an extruder, take plastic granules and mix in master batch (the colouring agent)
- Melt the mix and force it through a die to produce a continuous tube (called 'layflat')
- Take this layflat through a bag machine to seal and perforate each bag
- Pack a number of bags into a small cardboard container (or wrap them in a label)
- Pack off a number of these into a larger carton and label it.

Physically, on the shop floor, this will be done as one continuous process. But, in reality, I am carrying out two processes: I am making the layflat and processing it into bags, and I am then packing off those bags. (Remember also that I might use the same layflat to make bags of differing lengths, or to produce different pack sizes.)

So, rather than a single-level (flat) BOM that says I use granules, master batch and the various packaging items, it might make more sense to say that my finished product is made from layflat (as a sub-assembly) and that layflat is itself made from granules and master batch. This makes the BOM more understandable when I look at it and also makes the BOM for the layflat 're-usable' in that I can copy it to other product BOMs.

The bill of material structure

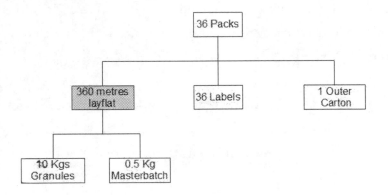

What MRP 'sees'

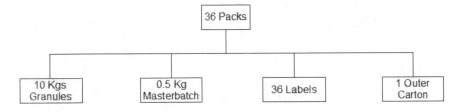

Obviously, in this simple example, this is not a big deal but imagine that you are in the automobile industry and that sub-assembly is an engine with hundreds of parts (we'll look at the sort of BOMs that an automobile maker might use later, as such companies have some interesting problems which are not entirely limited to their industry alone).

The ability to create re-usable building blocks within BOMs not only makes them easier and quicker to create; it also makes them easier to maintain. If a 'virtual sub-assembly' is used in many products, and a change is to be made, I can make it once in the phantom BOM rather than making it in, potentially, a large number of BOMs separately. I not only save time but I reduce the risk of forgetting to make some of the changes.

A phantom item is therefore something that I don't create a works order for and I don't put into stock. The layflat, once made, is immediately consumed by the next level up in the BOM. It only exists for a fleeting moment (hence the term 'phantom'). The term 'blow-through' part was coined because, when MRP is doing its calculations, it knows that works orders (or recommendations) are not required for these items and 'blows through' them to immediately consider the requirement for their components.

Phantom or not; a bill of material will hold, as a minimum, a quantity-required against each item (or component) listed on it. Some systems will also hold scrap rates so that MRP can take these into consideration (although these are, in some systems, held against the part number in the inventory master file. However, this is less beneficial as scrap rates for a component might well vary according to the item that it is being used in).

3.8 Routes (or Routings)

The routing has several functions, including:

- Informing the factory of detail of the work to be carried out.
- Allowing the work that it describes to be costed.
- Allowing the job to be tracked through its various stages.
- Making data available to capacity planning and capacity scheduling.

As the bill of material defines the materials or components that go into making an item, the routing defines the resource (generally labour and plant) that are required to produce it. Terminology will vary but a routing is generally made up of a number of operations (for example; Paint, Assemble, Test, Pack) although it is not impossible for a routing to have only one.

3.9 Bills of resource

Most ERP/MRPII/MRP systems hold bills of material and routings separately. Others view the two as being inseparable and have merged the two into one composite file. All that was said above about bills of material and routings holds true: effectively all that changes is the way the data is managed.

Whether a company should use separate BOM and routing files is not a debate that I intend to spend a lot of time on. Generally, ERP/MRPII/MRP systems are built one way or the other and the user doesn't get a choice. My personal preference is for separate files (though feel free to disagree with me) for the following reasons:

Within most (though not all) companies, the people who maintain bills of material are not the same people who maintain routings. It is preferable in ERP/MRPII/MRP systems for data to have only one owner: if multiple groups of people have the ability to change particular data there can be arguments over who changed what.

Over a period of time, routings and bills of material will legitimately change. New machines may be introduced and change the way things are made. Design changes may necessitate new components. For some companies, all that is necessary is to make the changes to the data and move on. For others, for example in aerospace or pharmaceuticals, it is necessary to maintain records of previous make or build specifications. These companies will hold several generations of routing and BOM data on their systems. Whereas companies in some industries can get away with holding a part 'revision' number on the stock master record, other industries find it easier or necessary to hold the revision indicator on the routing and BOM separately. In aerospace, for example, it is insufficient to say that you have made an item, or component, to a particular revision level: you have to be able to say that a particular revision of BOM was used and production took place using a specific revision of routing (which might be machine-specific). The number of records to be maintained in these circumstances is much-reduced when kept separately.

The above argument holds true when companies have alternative methods of manufacture. For example, some work may preferably be done on a CNC machine but may also be possible on a lathe when the CNC machine is heavily loaded. Holding routings and BOMs separately can make it easier to manage the number of permutations.

3.10 Works Orders

Works orders are a primary way of communicating requirements to the shop floor. In addition to holding data such as required date and quantity, works orders generally also hold a list of the materials required for their completion. Some manufacturing companies, when operating manual systems, just give the shop floor a copy of the bill of material (or parts list) but the works order goes further by multiplying component quantities by the works order quantity to give total quantity required. Additionally, a copy of the routing will be copied to the order.

Advantages of having works orders include:

- A pick list, showing components and quantities required, can be easily produced for the warehouse.
- Progress of the job through the production cycle can be recorded against the routing data.
- The works order serves as a collection point for costs as materials are issued and resource utilisation recorded.
- Detailed manufacturing instructions can, if necessary, be issued to the shop floor.

- Bills of material and routings can be easily amended for individual jobs; for example to use up obsolescent or obsolete components or to route the job through a different manufacturing process in the case of machine breakdowns.
- If the job is being manufactured to a different date than the MRP required date (as may happen if a job is brought forward to utilise spare capacity), the amended due date on the order can be read by MRP and components re-scheduled appropriately.

When using work orders, don't be tempted to raise and print them before they are actually needed. Some companies do this, and issue them to the shopfloor and the warehouse, but then things change. Perhaps the required date changes, or the quantity, or perhaps the bill of material gets amended. Getting back the original documentation whilst you issue new can be time-consuming and troublesome if it has been misfiled, and it is not at all uncommon for production to be duplicated in such circumstances.

But works orders may not always be required; for example if you have a continuous in-line process that pulls from bulk storage such as silos or you are operating kanbans. In these circumstances, you are unlikely to have material or process time variances so there is no real value in recording such data. Manufacturing being continuous, you don't need works orders to calculate work in progress values, and scheduling is generally not an issue.

True; you can, in these environments as in others, raise works orders and then backflush them (backflushing is a term used for a retrospective issue of components, based on bill of material quantities, when a completion is recorded against the order) but this can be a problem in a system that posts manufacturing costs to the ledgers only when the works order is finally closed out. You can get around the problem by raising daily works orders, even for a continuous process, but that can be wasteful in terms of operator time.

A better option is provided by systems that can backflush without the existence of a works order. The operator merely records the quantity of items produced and the system backflushes the components used: some systems will pause and let the operator make adjustments to components, quantities and through-put time before posting the transaction (this can be particularly useful if you are using batch traceability on some components or ingredients).

If you do use backflushing (with or without works orders) be aware that the component issues are retrospective. This means that, if you are doing a stock check, you will have used components without having transacted those issues in your stock file and this can cause apparent (but false) shortages. You need to cope with this procedurally to prevent causing yourself problems, particularly if you use cycle counting (perpetual inventory).

4.   How do I get it to work?

Whichever system you choose from the literally hundreds available on the market, no system is 'plug in and go'. All require more work than we frequently imagine to get to a stage where they can be switched on and become operational. We will look at the project management task later but, first, we will get down to basics and consider what the system needs from us and how we can satisfy its demands.

Let's consider first the 'static data' in the inventory file. By that I mean the data that, unlike elements such as on-hand quantities and costs, generally don't change. This data will be the bedrock on which the system stands and no time expended on getting it right is ever wasted.

4.1 Part numbers

The first and most obvious piece of data on the inventory record is the part number. Why am I bothering to discuss such a simple and straight-forward piece of information? Because some companies even get this part of a new system wrong. "How can a part number be wrong?", you ask. The main reason is that some companies have a different idea of what a part number is than an MRP system. A system generally believes in the rule of 'Form, fit and function'. That says that, for two items to share the same part number, they must be genuinely interchangeable and not just alternatives. The part number must uniquely identify the item that it is applied to (we will consider later how to cope with generic items in the system but for now will occupy ourselves with the 99% and not the exceptions).

From a design point of view, we might not care whether our bolts are zinc plated or not, and we might specify that an item is to be painted without worrying what colour but, if when we come to make and sell items, if these things matter, then plated and un-plated bolts cannot have the same part number and neither can paint have a generic part number. The reason is that a human being can look in a box and see how many bolts are plated and how many are not but a computer can't. Likewise, to a designer, a heat-treated casting is the same thing before and after heat treating, and can therefore have the same part number, but to a system the two are not interchangeable and so they can't. Mess with this rule at your peril.

This obviously can cause problems within an organisation. Designers and operations people having separate coding systems is clearly unsatisfactory. The problem is particularly acute when, for example, CAD systems are directly linked to MRP systems and bills of material released from the CAD system have some new components that are required to be automatically created in the latter system. MRPII can only buy and make 'real' parts. If 'Form, fit and function' are important, they simply have to be reflected in unique part numbers. Fast forward to when your system says 'Buy paint' and your buyer says 'What colour?'. Systems can't create information; they can only process what they are given. If it is truly necessary for you to use generic part numbers in your CAD system then you have to develop a procedure and process to replace these with 'proper' part numbers at the time of interface between the two systems.

We will look at this problem again later when considering bills of material but, in the meantime, let's just accept that a part number must uniquely specify the items that it is applied to. If you decide that, for whatever reason, this is something that you can't accept, then stop reading this book now and don't go down the MRP route: you will never get it to work properly for you.

Whilst thinking about part numbers, let's for a moment think also about their structure. Many of you will be moving from existing computerised systems where you already have part numbers in place. In these circumstances it is probably too late to think about changing them unless they are causing real problems. However; you may be a start-up or you may be a small company that has only previously had a computerised accounting system, so a discussion is perhaps warranted.

When it comes to part numbering systems, there are two schools of thought and, as with many other things in life, the best answer probably lies somewhere between the two. One school of thought says that part numbers should just start at '000001' and then go up sequentially. Every new item that has to be numbered just takes the next number in the sequence. The other school says that part numbers should be 'intelligent'; i.e. they should have a structure and should incorporate codes or text that help to identify the item to which they are applied. Let's look at the advantages and disadvantages of both approaches.

Firstly the sequential approach. The one obvious thing that it has going for it is simplicity. Creating a new number is merely a matter of going to a register and taking the next available number. Proponents of this approach argue that nowadays it is not necessary to group similar items into a part number range because modern systems have sufficient spare analysis fields to enable data to be analysed, and reports to be sorted, without sticking to a pre-set format. It is also argued that, as the company grows, it can never run out of part numbers: the worst that can happen is that you eventually have to stick an extra digit on to the end. On the other hand, it is undoubtedly true that it is easier to remember numbers if they have some sort of structure and a 'prompt' such as an initial character of 'C' for chemicals and 'F' for forgings (but what do you do then for castings?).

Devotees of the structured approach take this coding further (although sometimes to extremes—one example that I found was an electronics company that had 47-character part numbers where every character had a meaning). Their argument is that you don't have to remember part numbers because if you remember the 'rules' you can always work out what the number should be. They might say, for example, that the coding structure for a screw could be as follows:

- First character—'S' indicating a screw
- Second character indicating the material; e.g. 'B' for brass, 'S' for stainless steel etc
- Third character indicating 'P' for Philips, 'S' for slot head etc
- Fourth & fifth indicating width
- Sixth & seventh indicating length.

So, if I wanted a 4mm X 20mm brass, Philips-headed screw, I would ask for a SBP0420.

In the interests of simplicity, this example verges on over-simplification. Any screw expert would tell me that I have left some important criteria out. And that is my point. To do the job properly can take an unmanageable number of characters—remember the 47 characters? Even when trying to keep code lengths reasonable, companies generally need to apply codes to a whole range of items so the part number structure for, say, cable needs to be different from that for electric motors. In consequence, it is not just one set of coding rules that users have to learn but many and this, to some extent, invalidates or at least weakens the argument in their favour. In older systems, with inadequate spare analysis fields, there was a case for using structured part numbers so that data for a particular range of items could be extracted but those days are gone for all but the simplest systems.

Which system you go for depends largely on the number of part numbers you have to deal with; both now and in the future. As I said earlier, the best is probably somewhere between the two extremes. The fewer part numbers that you have, the simpler your part numbering system can be. My personal preference is for the first few characters to be meaningful but no more. One difficulty in structured codes is 'future proofing'; that is to say leaving sufficient character spaces to deal with all likely demand. For example; in my screw example, I had two characters to indicate screw length. What happens if, at some stage in the future, I have to introduce a screw of more than 99mm length? The one thing that we can be sure of in manufacturing is that we can be sure of nothing.

Two last tips when it comes to creating part numbers: firstly, if you are using both numeric and alpha characters in your codes, avoid using both zeros and letter 'O's. Likewise try to avoid using both the numeric '5' and the letter 'S': they can and will get confused. Also remember that the human brain likes to remember things in threes (I don't know why but it's true) so, particularly in the case of numeric codes or segments, try for lengths of three or six characters.

One last thought: if you think that your part number structure needs changing, this is the time to do it. You may think that your people will have enough to learn with a new system without having to learn new part numbers as well, but this will be your best chance for at least ten years to change your codes. If you don't change your codes, make sure it is a conscious decision and not just an oversight.

4.2 Lead times

I am going to consider purchasing and manufacturing lead times separately as different rules apply. Firstly let's consider purchasing lead times as, almost counter intuitively, although not in our control, they are the easiest to cope with. In my early days as a user of MRP systems, when someone asked me for purchasing lead times, I would get frustrated. The lead time on the same item from the same supplier could vary endlessly. Sometimes my supplier would have them in stock and sometimes I would be quoted a delivery of weeks or months.

The good news is that, in the case of purchasing lead times, accuracy doesn't really matter! How can I say that? Well; let's think of what the MRP system is going to do with those lead times. For simplicity, in the following example, let's talk in terms of seven day working weeks and let's also assume that MRP calculates that we need a delivery of items on the 30th of the month. If we have set a 7 day lead time, we will get a message that we need to order by the 23rd for delivery on the 30th. However, if we set a 14 day lead time, we will get a message to order by the 16th but, again, for delivery on the 30th—that is the key date. By exaggerating my lead time, all I am doing is giving my supplier more notice of my requirements; which is no bad thing.

Of course, there are three things that I have to consider:

1. If I put 'Delivery ASAP' on my Purchase Order, or if I allow my suppliers to deliver when they want and not when I want, the items can come in too early and that can give me cash flow and storage space problems. (You're not really paying your suppliers based on delivery date if they deliver early, are you?)

2. If I place the order early, even for delivery on the 30th, the world can change before I take delivery. I might have to go back to my supplier one or more times to reschedule the order. Obviously, the greater the time period between order and delivery, the greater chance that this will be necessary.

3. Lastly, with an exaggerated lead time, there will be occasions when the system applies that lead time and tells me to place the order at some time in the past. This, in truth, would be an irritant rather that a real problem. It just moves the requirement to the top of the pile, where I actually want it to be anyway.

So, within reason, I can afford to be pessimistic about my purchasing lead times. Notwithstanding the three points above, exaggerated purchasing lead times are not going to cause me cash flow or storage problems.

4.3 Manufacturing lead times.

Not so with manufacturing lead times, where exaggerated lead times can and will cause real damage.

Calculating realistic manufacturing lead times is a real problem. If we know how long it takes to manufacture 1,000 items then we know our manufacturing lead time; right? Actually; no. Even if you are in a process industry, where raw material is turned into product in one endless operation, you have problems.

The most obvious is that, unless you always have more capacity that you actually need, there will be times when you have to schedule operations on some jobs to be produced earlier that really needed. Although we are all focused on keeping down stocks, some buffer is required to ensure continuity. I know that some companies, e.g. in vehicle manufacture, can and do schedule hourly deliveries but their suppliers certainly can't.

The bigger problem, especially for companies that don't do continuous flow manufacturing, is that items generally go through a number of different processes, frequently on different machines or in different work centres. However much we try to fight against it, we are going to have queue times at those machines and work centres (indeed, if they are bottlenecks, we actually want to have queues to ensure that the facility runs at full potential and never stops). A particular job will therefore have to be started earlier than theoretically necessary to allow for those queues and, though it may then finish on-schedule, its actual time in process (its manufacturing lead time) will be extended. Beware, incidentally, of systems which only allow a fixed manufacturing lead time to be entered, regardless of manufacturing quantity.

Anyone with manufacturing experience knows that there is a world of difference between theoretical lead times and what can actually be achieved in real life. The temptation is then to 'take the pressure off' by being pessimistic. I know: I've done it myself. But, as opposed to exaggerated purchasing lead times, doing so can cause real problems.

Let's take an item that has a three-level bill of material and give each of those levels a one week manufacturing lead time. If the end item is due for delivery in week 20, the purchased items which go into the bottom level assembly must arrive in week 17. Now let's put in some 'safety time' to take the pressure off. We think that a one week manufacturing lead time is correct but we'll add an extra week to each, just to make sure that we will never be caught out by the unexpected. Now the purchased items at the bottom level will be scheduled in on week 14.

Does this matter? Well; the first thing that results is that, having taken delivery of the items earlier than is strictly necessary, you are likely to have to pay for them earlier than is strictly necessary. To an extent the payment terms that you have agreed with your suppliers come into play in any calculation: do you pay a number of days after the invoice date or do you pay at the end of the month following delivery, for example? To keep the mathematics simple in the following example, let's assume that delivery 3 weeks early means payment 3 weeks early, as that is likely to be the average whatever you do.

We'll take a company with a purchasing spend of £50 million. They are pretty much average with their raw material stock turns, as having to order some items in minimum batch sizes and having bought against forecasts that didn't firm up, have given them a raw material stock of £2 million (about 2 weeks usage). Bringing in stock 3.weeks early then increases their stock by 3 weeks, and they now have 5 weeks' worth and have two problems to consider. One is that they now have to finance an extra £3 millions' worth of stock, and the second is that the amount of stock that they are required to hold has more than doubled, so the amount of storage space that they need also doubles.

Obviously, in this example, I am assuming that they are starting off from a good position in only having two weeks' worth of stock to begin with. Depending on the industry that you are in, and how good your existing controls are before you implement MRP, these figures could fluctuate dramatically up or down. I leave it to you to do the mathematics using your own data. You may well already have exaggerated manufacturing lead times in your current system and, by reflecting these in the new system also, you would just be maintaining the status quo. However, even then you are missing out on an opportunity, as reducing stock levels is, if not a target for new MRP systems (and it definitely should be), at least a common result of a good MRP system that has been properly implemented. More on this later.

So, having established that realistic manufacturing lead times, that allow for the unexpected but not excessively so, are vital, how do we do the hard part of establishing just what they should be? Well, the most obvious starting point is actual experience. You probably have a good feel for how long things take, or at least should take. You know that getting manufacturing lead times down is a good thing for a number of reasons, including the following:

Firstly, if you get your manufacturing lead times down, you get your delivery lead times down. That makes you a more attractive supplier and can be expected to result in an increased market share. At worst, if your competitors are also working to get their delivery lead times down, it will maintain your competitiveness.

Secondly, getting them down will have a major impact on your work in progress volumes and values. That will positively impact on your costs and profitability.

The point that I am making is that, although the status quo might have to be the place to start, it shouldn't ever be considered as being acceptable. If, for whatever reason, you start there, load those figures to the new system with a determination, and a structured plan (not a vague wish) to reduce them.

The second option, especially if the data that you currently have is inaccurate or incomplete, is to take an iterative approach. Start off with your best guess and measure reality against that; continually refining your values until you are comfortable with them. To ensure continuity of supply, you might initially have to be pessimistic, as having too much stock in the short term is better than running out and then having line shortages and unhappy customers. Don't therefore react immediately when one works order comes through faster than expected: wait until you have enough data to feel confident that there is a pattern. The danger with this approach, of course, is that you will take your eye of the ball and, once entered, such values become set in stone. That is also the reason that I suggest having a continual process of reviewing manufacturing lead times and developing ways of getting them down.

One final word of warning: reduced lead times result in reduced stock levels but reduced stock levels do not result in reduced lead times! So make sure that you approach the problem and opportunity from the right angle.

4.4 Queue lengths

In the previous section, we said that queue lengths, and therefore times, may be inevitable however hard we try to reduce them. Let's briefly justify that statement before we move on.

Firstly, let's look at unavoidable queues: the ones that we can fight to reduce but probably will never completely eradicate. If we can understand what causes these, we can at least reduce them even if we can't totally eliminate them.

One major problem is that, unless you have a continuous-flow process operation, a particular work centre can be fed from multiple other work centres, each of which we want to be working at the maximum possible efficiency. That, however, means that they are operating at different speeds or output rates. Different jobs on the same machine take different amounts of time. Another way of looking at it is to say that some machines and jobs consume materials and sub-assemblies faster than others.

In an ideal world, we would have batch sizes of one and the problem would shrink to insignificance. But people in manufacturing have to be pragmatic and deal with reality. We can't achieve perfection but, if we aim for the stars, we might at least reach the moon. So our target has to be continually working to reduce our batch sizes even if we can never get them to one. Let's then look at why batch sizes are frequently bigger than we would want them to be.

Firstly, the killer—set-up time. Any Production Manager wants to maximise machine run times for maximum productivity. Set-up time is non-productive time and the easy way to reduce set-up time is to reduce the number of set-ups. That means that, when we set up a machine, instinctively we want that machine to run for as long as possible before we stop it for another set-up. That means big batches. Ways of reducing set-up times are beyond the remit of this book so will not be considered in any detail. Suffice to say that they include:

- Redesigning jigs and tools so that they can be changed-out more speedily (with a target called SMED—single minute exchange of dies).
- More use of 'standard parts'. For example, I once had a car that was not the top of the range and didn't have all of the toys on the dashboard that more-expensive models had. It had, however, space for those extras and blanking plates for where they would go. The result was that the car maker had one dashboard instead of two (or more), Clever design, where the designer understands the practicalities of manufacture, can make an enormous difference. When did you last speak to your designers about problems and opportunities and ask for their help?

- Last but not least—better planning! That results in fewer 'rush jobs', where machines are torn down for priority jobs to be rushed through, only to be re-instated for the rest of the batch to be completed. (Should the rest of the batch always be completed? Quite possibly not.)

Secondly, Economic Order Quantities (EOQ). We have mentioned these before, and railed against them, but they deserve more criticism. Like many bad ideas, they started as a good one. The idea was to find a way of trading off the inventory cost of large batches against the accumulated set-up costs of the number of smaller batches required for the same quantity of output. Mathematically it is fine, perhaps even elegant, but it was always a tool that required to be applied intelligently and, alas, it hasn't always been.

As a way of balancing set-up and stocking costs, it doubtless works but there are important things that it ignores or over-looks.

For example, it considers the stocking cost, but only from a very simplistic point of view: that of the cost of the money tied up in that stock (which it applies as a percentage). What it doesn't, and probably can't, accurately reflect is the cost of storage space. If I put a pallet load of electronic devices into a store alongside a pallet load of cardboard boxes, then the cost of storage of each is the same but, as a percentage of their cost, is wildly different. The storage area or volume that an item takes up is rarely proportionate to its value. I don't know of any variant of EOQ that can deal with that.

Furthermore, at times when we don't have excess capacity, we can be sure that when we are making items that are not immediately required, we are doing so at the expense of not making items that we do want. In those circumstances the cost of the resultant shortages far outweighs any saving in set-up cost. EOQ is a very blunt instrument. Use it if you must but use it with extreme caution, knowing the damage that it can do.

One last word of warning about EOQ is justified. EOQ may tell us (although it probably won't; as discussed above) an optimum batch size but it doesn't stop to consider whether or not we actually need the full quantity that it is suggesting. The danger of making stock that we don't need is very real (to say nothing of the dangers that are also added to the mix if we are making items with finite shelf lives).

So, if we are not to use EOQ but we can't have batch sizes of one because we still have set-up times that are unavoidable, what can we do? Having seen that basing decisions on crude financial criteria are unlikely to give us sensible answers, let's think of other criteria. The two that come most immediately to mind are space and time.

When it comes to space, some of us (particularly in process industries) already have batch sizing rules. In process industries, what gets made frequently has to go into holding containers, tanks or silos. A batch size is obvious and unavoidable because, if we make more than that, we have a mess on the floor. With other items that can be held in a regular warehouse, storage area or volume is not such an obvious limitation but perhaps it should be. Perhaps a walk around your storage areas is a good idea—are some items taking up an inordinate amount of storage space? I once worked in a factory where we used cardboard tubes in the manufacturing process. They were cheap so EOQ wanted large quantities but the space that they took up was disproportionate to their value and an 'economic' quantity would have filled the warehouse. Knowing what space you can spare for an item gives you a pretty good idea of what your maximum (though not optimum) batch size should be.

A better option is frequently to use time as a limiting factor. Again, with shelf life items, it is self-evident that we shouldn't make four weeks' worth of items that have a one week shelf life but the concept could and should be applied to other items also. In calculating whether we should make one days' worth of stock, or one week or one month, then pragmatically we will consider some of the points mentioned above:

We may be restrained by the amount of storage space that we can, or want to, make available for the finished batch.

The cost of the items will come into play: I might be happy to make a months' worth of washers but not of crankshafts.

Whilst not being driven by set-up time, I will want to ensure that the quantities that I come up with are not silly. As with anything else in the world of MRP, make sure that the result of whatever you do is checked by a sensible, knowledgeable human being before handing over authority to the system.

4.5 Bulk issue items

These can also be called expensed items or free-issue items. The concept is not as widely used as it should be so it is worth a mention.

MRP systems will have a way of flagging these items, generally on the stock record but occasionally on the bill of material. The idea of such a flag is to take these items out of MRP control. Now why would I want to spend a lot of time and money introducing an MRP system just to turn it off for some items? The answer is that, with most items, I want to transact all movements, including issues to works orders. But there are some items that are so cheap that the cost of transactions can be greater than the cost of the items themselves. Falling into this category for many companies are items such as staples, screws, washers, dowels, resistors etc, where the cost of such items issued to a particular job can amount to pennies. To issue these to particular jobs is a nonsense but let me quote a real-life example to prove my point.

An electronics company did not embrace the concept and, when a job was released to the shopfloor, a storeman religiously counted all of the necessary components into boxes as he was kitting-up the job. Frequently, during the assembly operation, the operator would be short of a few components. Did the storeman mis-count? Did a tiny component get lost at the bottom of the box or drop on the ground? There was no way of telling but they did have a shortage that had to be addressed so, to get replacements out of stock, a requisition was raised and signed-off by the department foreman so that new items could be correctly re-issued. On analysis, it was found that the value of items on such a requisition averaged seven pence—not seven pence each but seven pence per requisition.

This is clearly nonsense and totally un-justifiable. Bulk issue items avoid this madness. They are purchased and stored in the normal way but are issued by the container, box or bottle to the shopfloor as and when the previous issue runs out. For example, a box of staples will get issued to a department or individual operator (and not a specific job) and the full issue quantity will be transacted out of stock at that point. MRP picks the item up when it hits a reorder point (ROP). I have heard nonsensical arguments against this approach but let's just spend a few minutes knocking them down, one by one:

- Unless all items are issued to a job, there is no accurate cost for the completed item. I am not advocating that expensive items be bulk issue items; we are talking about items that cost pennies so, unless the end item costs pennies also (in which case see the section on backflushing), they really don't matter. Many systems will, in any case, allow the cost of the theoretical usage of such items to be posted to unit cost automatically anyway.

- We can't have accurate stock control if we don't transact issues to works orders at the same time as they happen. Yes you can! And the results will be better. Issue small components in less that container quantities and the only way to limit count errors is to issue by weight but, when item weight falls to less that the weight of a washer, you can forget 100% accuracy anyway. That says that you have to count items individually, at which point the cost of the transaction can be greater than the cost of the items transacted.

- Ah, yes! But if we issue a box of 1000 washers, rather than just the 48 that we need, we are not accurately controlling stock because we really do have the remaining 952. That's true, but does it matter? What is the cost of a box of washers?

- But if we don't tightly control the number of items that we issue, our staff might steal them! Two questions: do you really care about a handful of washers? I'm sure that there are better things to steal on your factory floor. Secondly; why are you employing people that you don't trust?

Many companies nowadays don't even try to control trivial items. They will have a help-yourself rack of such items in the shopfloor and a trusted supplier will come in regularly to top it up; charging for the replenishment quantity. If you don't trust your suppliers (why are you using them, then?), it is easy to track what you are being charged for against what you think you should be using (or against historic usage).

One last thought: when the cost of control surpasses the cost of the items being controlled, the lunatics have truly taken over the asylum.

4.6 Bills of Material

We have already noted that a company can have multiple versions of their bills of material. It is not uncommon for Design, Costing and Production to have different bills and I guess that, in some companies, we could add the spares department to the list. We have also previously mentioned planning bills, that allow forecasts at a family level to be processed and we will look later at configurable bills. All of these have a purpose but it is the Production bill of material that MRP uses so it is that that we will focus on. The rest may well co-reside on our system but are not used by it, except maybe for enquiry and reporting purposes.

In essence, though, a bill of material defines not only the components that go into an item but also the way that the item is put together, in terms of the assemblies and sub-assemblies that go into it. We can have different revisions of bills and may, regardless, modify a bill for a particular production run. Until we specifically choose a different revision or modify the bill at a works order level, MRP will use what we have specified as being the current bill. Some MRP systems give us the ability to hold effectivity dates against bills so that MRP can apply forthcoming editions of the bill to future requirements as appropriate.

It is normally the case that bills are 'multi-level' (see an example of that in Fig. 4 in section 4.11.3) even if some of the items in these are phantoms. One obvious question is how many levels a bill of material should have? As few as possible, is the easy answer but, before we try to establish what that means, let's justify the statement.

What problems do excessive layers cause?

- Excessive layers mean a lot more effort is required to enter bills to the system and to maintain them thereafter. If you double the number of bills in your system then generally speaking you are doubling your workload. Some companies don't stop at just doubling their workload: I found one that used a twelve-level bill for making office chairs.
- Each of the extra bills has to have its own part number. That means more work and a bigger stock file, as well as a bigger bills of material file.
- You will (unless you make wide use of phantom items) need a lot more works orders to process all of these additional parts into and out of stock. That means a lot more transactions to

be reported to the system (and a lot more paperwork to be generated by it).

- Bigger inventory, bills of material and works order files will impact on your MRP run times. Bigger files take longer to process. This may not be a big problem if you run MRP overnight but I have a number of companies who welcome the opportunity to run MRP updates over lunch as well as overnight so, for them, keeping run times down is important.

- More data and more transactions mean more chance of error. Try as we might, we will never eradicate all errors but I think it is reasonable to assume that increasing data entry and transactions also increases errors.

- Keeping the big one until last: excessive levels on your bills can have a disastrous effect on your manufacturing lead times. I joined one outfit that had been advised by an international consultancy to have what I would regard as an excessive number of levels in their bills, in the belief that they would achieve more accurate costing (they didn't). The production lead time on key sub-assemblies went out to 19 days. There wasn't time for us to rebuild all of the bills (which would have markedly reduced MRP run times) so we phantomised most of them and lead times dropped to 5 days. The extra 14 days had been taken up by paperwork processing. Unbelievable but true.

Having warned you off having an excessive number of layers in your bills, let me also warn you off having too few. Levels are there for a purpose. They let sub-assemblies be planned and made in a controlled fashion. The assemblies and sub-assemblies that go into the final item will generally all make their separate ways through your production processes. They will have differing start and finish dates so cannot usefully all be lumped together. Although each separate work order may go through several different processes and work centres in its life, there is an advantage to being able to track and cost each individually. Use of the routing module (see section 3.8) enables us to do that without resort to crazy numbers of works orders.

In reaching a balance between the advantages of an increased number of bills (and therefore works orders) and the previously mentioned advantages of a smaller number, we have to remember that information has a value but it also has a cost. Whatever advice I give here must be to some extent or other generic, given that some readers will be making ice cream and others will be making airliners. However, most organizations that I have worked with operate quite happily and successfully on bills that have no more than three or four levels. If you think that you need more than that, remember that Concorde was built with a five level bill of material although, in fairness, the Space Shuttle did take six. Do you really then need twelve levels for a chair? Really?

Getting back to basics; a bill of material, whether for an end product, an assembly or a sub-assembly, will contain the following data as a minimum:

- the part numbers of the items that make it up (its 'children')
- the quantities of those items that are required for one unit of measure of the parent. By that I mean that, if you are building washing machines, you probably have a unit of measure of something like 'EACH' for the washing machine and the

number of items specified on the bill will be the number required to make one washing machine. But if you are making wine, you might have a case of twelve bottles as a unit of measure and the bill of material would specify twelve bottles, twelve labels etc.

Some systems will allow other items of information to be held, such as:

- the drawing number or specification reference that the item is being built against
- anticipated scrap percentages for the parent item
- anticipated scrap percentages for each child (component)
- an offset for each component (i.e. the number of days into the build that this component is required). For example, if it takes three days to build something, the packing case is probably not required until day three.
- etc.

They may also allow quantities to be expressed in a unit of measure that is not the normal stocking unit of measure for that item. As an example, I have worked with pharmaceutical manufacturers who buy ingredients in tonnes but whose bills of material must be set at an individual tablet level. Some tablets contain barely a trace element of some ingredients, so expressing their quantities in decimals of a tonne would be painful if not nonsensical.

In considering bills of material, we have to remember that computer systems are not intelligent. In the words of Charles Babbage in the 19th Century, when writing of his Analytical Engine:

"The Analytical Engine has no pretensions whatever to originate anything. It can do whatever we know how to order it to perform."

That means that they must be given, by us, all of the data that they need to do their calculations. If the bills of material are incomplete or wrong, then the recommendations that MRP makes will also be incomplete or wrong. Over to Mr Babbage again; and again talking about his Analytical Engine:

"On two occasions I have been asked, "Pray, Mr Babbage, if you put into the machine wrong figures, will the right answer come out?" I am not able rightly to apprehend the kind of confusion of ideas that could provoke such a question."

I guess we would now say, "Garbage in, garbage out". Perhaps less eloquent; but rather more succinct.

In real life, this can give us a problem when we are dealing with a new product or a re-designed item. Frequently we will know that a new bill of material is required long before we know exactly what needs to be on that bill. The specification of the item may not be complete because of a range of reasons, including:

- awaiting a design decision ("What size of engine will we need to power this?")
- awaiting a customer decision ("Do I want it in red or white?")
- awaiting a marketing decision ("What sort of packaging should we have?")

The list goes on. I have been told since my first experiences with MRP that bills of material should not go onto the system until they are complete and I took this advice for many years. But, in moving to the aircraft industry, I started to find the problems that this approach resulted in to be unbearable.

Many of our raw materials were on long lead times (up to six months) but the period between the design being firmed up and the customer requiring delivery were very much shorter. When I arrived at the company, they were trying to manage the problem by human memory, post-it notes and spreadsheets and it wasn't working. None of them were reliable and every time they let us down, they let us down badly.

The answer was to ignore all that the text books told us: incomplete bills **should** go onto the system to allow us to order long lead time items even before the design is firmed-up (as long as the use of such items has been firmed up!). But how then to remember all of the things that had to be continually chased up?

We created a range of 'reminder' part numbers such as, Z001 Awaiting design decision, Z002 Awaiting customer decision, etc. (these examples are for simplicity's sake—we actually had subdivisions of these codes).

All of these part numbers had lead times that related to the expected purchasing lead time of such items. When an incomplete bill of material went onto the system, it went with whatever 'reminder' part numbers were required. This gave us two great benefits: firstly every time we ran MRP, the output generated reminders with decision-required dates. Secondly, also every week, we ran a 'Where used' report against these codes and that gave us a consolidated list of all outstanding decisions. This report was then given to the bodies responsible for making decisions or getting answers.

Result? Nothing got lost or forgotten. We possibly upset a few MRP purists along the way but sometimes the end justifies the means.

4.7 Planning bills

We have already said that, for some companies, forecasting sales orders is very difficult but nevertheless essential because of extended lead times but we also said that The Law of Big Numbers can help. So how do we use The Law of Big Numbers?

Let's imagine that we are building a car. That car comes with a number of choices. I can have:

- a 1.2 or 1.6 litre petrol or 1.9 litre diesel engine
- a manual or automatic gearbox
- a 3 or 5 door, or an estate car body shell
- in silver, white, red or black paint
- with upholstery in black, grey or brown.

Whether I am Fiat, Ford, Volkswagen or whoever, I am unlikely to know how many 1.6 litre, five door automatics in red with grey upholstery that I am going to sell next week. But I might have a reasonable idea of how many cars in total that I am going to sell and experience might tell me that:

- 20% of the cars that I sell use the 1.2 litre engine, 30% the 1.6 and 50% the diesel
- 90% use the manual gearbox and 10% the auto box
- etc, working down the choices list.

If I then create a composite bill of material that reflects those percentages and feed in a forecast at the model level of, say 10,000 cars, my MRP system will tell me that I need:

- 2,000 1.2 litre petrol engines
- 3,000 1.6 litre petrol engines
- 5,000 1.9 litre diesel engines
- 9,000 manual gearboxes
- 1,000 automatic gearboxes
- etc.

I will never build a car with 0.9 of a manual gearbox and 0.1 of an automatic box but the point is that I will have provisioned, reasonably accurately, for actual orders when they come in. From that perspective, I don't care how all of the options go together on any individual car because that is not important to me at this stage. I just know that the items that I have procured are likely to satisfy my production demand.

By moving my forecast to a higher level, I am dealing with bigger numbers and getting better, safer and more-reliable results.

4.7.1 Configuration Bills of Material / Product Configurators

So far, we have looked at regular bills of material and planning bills of material. There is a third type: one that fulfils a very specific function and is not commonly found in packaged systems, although it is increasingly available as an add-on. That is the configuration bill of material.

Most things in this world move in cycles and we are definitely in a phase where the customer is king. No longer can manufacturing companies tell their customers that they can have any colour they like as long as it is black. There is too much competition out there and, in many industries, there is too much capacity. The result is that many companies cannot afford other than to give customers what they want. We have already mentioned the proliferation of options and extras in the automobile industry, which are such that it is now unusual for any two consecutive cars on the production line to be the same, particularly now when fewer car companies can afford to make to stock.

But this changing business paradigm affects many other industries, not least the upholstered furniture trade. A number of years back, it was common at the top end of the trade for the customer to have multiple options available to them when they went to buy a new suite but these choices have worked their way down market as companies feel the need to be flexible. Choices available to customers now frequently include:

- settee size (two, three or four seater)
- chair size (ladies or gents)

- cushion interior (feather or foam)
- colour of wood facings

as well as a choice of dozens if not hundreds of fabrics. One company that I worked with recently not only offered a wide range of fabrics and colours, but allowed customers to choose a different option for every panel. Cushions could be a different fabric and colour than the arms, and could be different colours and fabrics on the reverse. This poses challenges both at the order entry stage and at the manufacturing stage. How do we ensure that the choices were all captured correctly and how do we ensure that this is done in a way that allows a systematic approach to manufacture? A look at another furniture maker demonstrates the problem and solution.

This company makes office chairs: not exactly rocket science then. However, when the customer orders a chair, a number of questions become necessary, beyond the obvious one of "Which model?" Armed with that initial piece of information, the sales clerk has to follow up with a range of questions, including:

- in leather or fabric?
- what colour?
- with castors or glides?
- with or without arms?
- with or without a writing tablet?

Now my options become more difficult, as I can't have the writing tablet if I chose not to have arms. And the choice of fabric might enforce fire-resistant foam in the back and seat, rather than the regular foam filling. How is the sales clerk to be guided through the choices process in such a way that the final configuration is not only what the customer wants but is also viable from a manufacturing perspective? How do I ensure that the writing tablet cannot be specified unless arms have been? Last but by no means least, how do I ensure that the customer has been charged, and charged correctly, for their choices: that they paid extra for the chrome base but less for having the glides rather than the castors?

Previously the company relied on experienced sales clerks but, inevitably, new clerks made mistakes and these mistakes upset customers and cost money to rectify. Furthermore, in the days when they made dozens of chairs, it was possible to print off each order as text and give it to the factory as a job instruction. In those days, fabric was on a re-order point so fabric issues were practically on a 'help yourself' basis and, though no look-ahead as would be provided by MRP was possible, the company could cope with the waste and inefficiency that resulted. As the dozens of orders changed to hundreds, such manual methods ceased to be viable and increasingly broke down. Consequently, order processing costs began to rise steeply.

At this stage, with a new MRP system en route, the company approached its software provider for a solution and a 'Sales Order Configurator' was specified. This took all of the options out of the heads of experienced and knowledgeable people and systematised it as a set of rules that the computer could understand and apply. The sales clerks are now guided through the process. As individual decisions are taken, other decisions are enforced or excluded according to the rules.

None of this is easy, of course. Although the software provider had installed configurators before, and some re-usable code therefore existed already, the rules are unique and specific to each customer. It was not just a case of getting the rules right, but of getting all of the necessary data out of people's heads and into the system. The configuration bills need to hold costs as well as options and are necessarily complex. Getting the system right was a long and arduous process but was ultimately worthwhile as now the company is having to deal with fewer mistakes and the sales clerks are having to deal with fewer unhappy customers: an example of a computer system producing a win-win situation or, if the customers are included, a win-win-win situation!

4.8 Routings

As we mentioned before, routings have several purposes in MRPII:

- They provide information to the shop floor on the activities to be performed
- They provide the capacity planning and scheduling systems with data for their calculations
- They enable work in progress tracking to be performed
- They provide data that enables products to be costed.

They frequently also hold information on activities that are sub-contracted.

Except in some process industries, where raw materials are turned into finished product in one continuous flow, routings generally are made up of a number of operations. Each of these operations will have, as a minimum, the following data held against it:

- The resource used. Sometimes this will just be a machine type (eg saw, lathe, oven etc) or a labour category (machinist, painter, inspector etc). In the case of the labour category, in factories which have considerable flexibility of similarly costed labour, I have seen just the one category (eg Operator) used quite happily. There are obviously instances when a particular operation requires both labour and a machine and most systems allow for this. If a machine has an operator full-time, and this operator is not moved to another machine when there is insufficient work, some system will allow the operator and machine to be viewed as one entity and scheduled and costed accordingly.

- A description of the activity being performed.

- The amount of time that is required to carry out that activity. This may include several elements such as:

  ◦ Set-up time. This would be a fixed amount of time to, for example, set up a jig or adjust a machine. In these circumstances the time will not vary according to the quantity of items to be produced.

  ◦ Run time. This will be an amount of time per item (eg one hour each) or fixed-size batch of items (eg one thousand per hour). Care should be taken in choosing or setting up a system in circumstances where you have, for example, one operator looking after several machines. Many systems cannot cope well with this and imaginative work-arounds may be required.

  ◦ Clean-down time. As with set-up, this is generally a fixed amount of time. (When I say that, I am saying that the time taken to set up or clean down a machine is fixed for a particular job on a particular machine; not that the activity takes the same amount of time on all machines and all jobs.)

In some industries it is also necessary to have 'Delay' time; for example to allow paint to dry or to allow an oven to cool down before items can be removed. Likewise, it may be necessary to recognise 'move time' if the items have to be moved a substantial distance (e.g. to a sub-contractor or off-site facility) for the next operation to be performed.

Some systems allow more information to be held, such as:

- Tooling requirements
- If the operation is sub-contracted out, details of sub-contractors, prices etc
- Scrap or yield, so that a capacity planning tool can recognise that subsequent operations will take place against a reduced quantity.

Generally, when something gets made, it goes through a number of operations. A work instruction (as opposed to a routing) may well need to have very detailed directions and, though these can easily be held in most systems, it is generally impractical and unnecessary to have them as separate operations on a routing; although some systems have 'milestone operations' so that progress need only be reported at specified gateways, with other operations being 'assumed' to have happened.

At its simplest, I have seen companies operate happily with routings that say, effectively, "Make it in the factory" but this is unusual for a number of reasons:

- Most items will pass through multiple work centres, or departments, and these will commonly have differing costing rates: a CNC machine will have a different cost per hour than a lathe and an autoclave will have a different cost per hour than a shrink-wrap tunnel, as examples.
- With only one operation on the routing, it is hard to track which stage a particular job is at.
- Capacity planning and scheduling can only then work at a factory level, making them useless in all but the simplest of environments.

To make routings useful and usable, then, they need to be reasonably detailed but not excessively so. It is not possible to give precise guidelines on how many operations a routing should have, as they will vary from industry to industry, but we can say that if consecutive operations take place within the same work centre or department, it is unlikely that there will be any advantage to having them as separate operations on the routing. Additionally, if an operation takes very little time to perform (for an average production batch size), having it on the routing is probably not worth the effort unless your system offers the 'milestone' facility previously mentioned. This goes against the grain for people, who want very tight control and very precise costing but, as we said previously, information has a cost as well as a value. Entering transactions into a system costs time and money: is it worth spending five pounds to know that a ten pounds operation has happened, or should it just not be assumed to have happened?

4.9 Sub-contract operations

It may appear obvious what I mean by sub-contracting but, for the purpose of dealing with it in an MRP system, it is worth looking at various types of sub-contracting in order to decide how they fit in. This section comes very deliberately after bills of material and routings as, in most systems, they are very closely linked.

One type of sub-contracting is where I design something (whether a component, sub-assembly or finished item) and sub-contract its manufacture, in its entirety, to a sub-contractor. The sub-contractor is then responsible for sourcing any raw materials or components required and for delivering to me the completed item.

At the other extreme, I provide the sub-contractors, either from my stocks or direct from my suppliers, with all of the materials needed so that their responsibility is only for supplying labour, machine time etc. Sometimes they will return a completed item to me but frequently I will have subcontracted only one or some of the operations on the routing. These operations may take place at any place on the routing, from specialist machining at the beginning through to mandatory certification testing at the end.

In the middle of these two extremes sits the grey area so beloved of manufacturing; the area that means that we have to have multiple tool sets in order to do a comprehensive job.

Looking at the first scenario, where we supply the sub-contractors with designs or specifications and they supply manufactured items, we find ourselves having a debate: are these sub-contracted items or are they purchased items that just happen to have been made to our specification? I think they are the latter.

When we manufacture something internally, the bill of material and the routing have important functions that are irrelevant when the sub-contractor is doing all the work. We will not be issuing parts or ingredients so we don't need the bill of material in order to create a pick list for the warehouse, and we don't need MRP to have provisioned them in the first place either. We will not be tracking progress as the items move through the sub-contractor's processes so we don't need a routing. Granted we will need to know, as a company, what goes into the items that are made for us but we will have this information in our design systems so is it worth duplicating it in our MRP system when MRP is not going to do anything with it? In instances where a sub-contractor is doing something at a pre-agreed fixed price, it is hard to see a justification for incurring the expense involved in setting up and maintaining bills of material and routes.

There is one exception that I have come across that may be valid. That was with a company whose sub-contractors had to buy raw materials in a volatile market place and who, in consequence, wanted to have prices reviewed frequently. By holding bills of materials on their system, and current costs on their stock file, they were able to re-value their items (some systems call this a 'cost roll-up') regularly to establish fair prices for their sub-contractors. How accurate these material current costs were, given that the company never actually bought them, is however open to question and I can certainly think of better ways of solving the problem, such as the customer paying the suppliers material costs separately. In general then; if sub-contractors are providing their own materials, the items that they deliver should be viewed as purchased items.

Moving up one level of complexity; what if I provide some or all of the materials that the sub-contractor requires? In this case, the answer may be that we are constrained by the software that we are using. The sub-contractor's lead time is also an important factor: i.e. the length of time between issuing material to the sub-contractor and receiving the items that have consumed that material. Are we happy that material issued to a sub-contractor can be viewed immediately as work in progress (and posted there in the accounts) or do we issue such materials to the sub-contractor in bulk and view them as stock until we have had confirmation that they have been consumed? I see no advantage to this unless materials can be pulled back from the sub-contractor for alternative use.

The best approach is generally to issue the material out of your stock and, at an accounting level, post it to a sub-contractor WIP (work in progress) account; then do the contra posting in the accounts when doing the receipt transaction of the manufactured item. Some systems will cope with the accounting element of this better than others but the worst case would be that your accounting people will have to post a few journals to the General Ledger each month. If this seems onerous, ask yourself how much more money the company will make or save by going down the detailed BOM and route path. If what you are doing isn't saving you money or making you money, it is costing you money so why are you doing it? (Will the first person to say "For better management information" please stand in front of the firing squad? If you don't deserve to be shot, you at least deserve to be fired.)

The most complex scenario, and one that causes difficulties in some systems, is when the sub-contractor is not delivering back to me an item to go into stock, but an item that requires further processing before it becomes a stockable item. As previously mentioned, more than one operation on the routing may be sub-contracted and, where multiple operations are involved, they might be carried out by more than one sub-contractor. In these circumstances, it may be necessary to provide documentation such as pick lists and delivery notes so that items can be moved to, and between, sub-contractors. It will also be necessary to gather the sub-contract operation costs onto a works order along with costs that were incurred in-house so that we get a complete and accurate view of the completed item.

It is normally the case that the sub-contractors will require a purchase order to cover their elements of work and most systems will allow this order to be linked to its parent works order so that costs flow through automatically. Occasionally, companies have such close relationships with their sub-contractors that purchase orders are not required for each element of work. Sometimes a 'call off' order is raised and sometimes not even that. It is important, however, that these costs get onto the works order and, if your WIP tracking system lacks the 'milestone' option mentioned earlier (see section 4.8), it may be necessary to set your sub-contractor up as an internal department, tracking it accordingly, and posting monthly journals to your General Ledger to bring the financial aspects into line periodically.

4.10 Consignment stock

Consignment stock can be our stock held at customers' premises or supplier stock held at ours. It is this latter stock that we are considering here, although the answers discussed can easily be extrapolated into the former.

Most MRPII systems don't cope very well with consignment stock and many don't address it at all. The reason is that commercial systems are aimed at multiple customers, or potential customers, and there is no universally accepted way of handling such stock. A quick look at how some companies handle supplier consignment stock will prove my point.

I had one company that had an excellent relationship with a particular supplier. They had dealt with each other for so long and so well that they had transcended the normal customer/supplier relationship and had become trading partners. So much so that they trusted each other and, though their respective auditors insisted on checks, they had reached a stage in their trading relationship where neither expected to be cheated by the other (nor were they). Whereas most companies view consignment stock as moving costs along the supply chain (generally from customer to supplier), these two companies saw an opportunity to take costs *out* of the supply chain with a symbiotic relationship. It worked as follows.

Both customer and supplier knew which products contained the supplier's components, and in what quantities (don't forget that they trusted each other, and checks were in place). When the customer despatched a product, it had to have been delivered with the supplier's components built in. A weekly report showed the supplier content of the week's despatches and they were immediately paid for. At any time, the quantity of consignment stock at the customer was the total sent there minus the quantity paid for, and periodic stocktakes easily confirmed this. With visibility of available stock, and information on projected usage, it was easy for the supplier to maintain stock at agreed levels.

In this example of consignment stock, the customer never actually owned it as it went straight from supplier-owned stock to an accounting cost of sale. Their only challenge was to ensure that the costs were included in their product costs so that profitability reports were accurate and the cost of sale calculation was accurate. This is easy for companies that operate Standard Costing but, as they were operating an Actual Costing system, they were able, in the system that they operated, to add these costs as an 'extra' on the bill of material: most systems have a way of facilitating this. From the supplier perspective, the stock remained theirs until they had been advised that it had been used; at which point they merely invoiced it and, because the updates were regular, they had no problems in maintaining stock.

The above example worked well because both parties trusted each other and because the transparency of the methodology made it easy for checks to be carried out and auditors satisfied. It is always necessary to have a degree of trust when operating consignment stock but perhaps this is extreme.

Other examples of consignment stock operations that I have worked with use secure or defined storage areas to reinforce trust. Typically there will be an area of the customer's warehouse that is given over to the supplier's stock. That area will maintain an agreed stock level but the stock within it remains the supplier's until it is moved out. In the meantime, it remains on the supplier's stock records, enabling stock checks to be taken at any time for verification purposes. Customers who operate this way then 'purchase' the stock as moves over the boundary into their area of the warehouse. This can be easily achieved by setting up a call-off purchase order and transacting receipts against it. Frequently the supplier will be given copies of the subsequent system-generated receipt notes (though more-usefully a consolidated computer-generated report) so that their stock system can be updated and sales invoices raised.

There is a balance to be found here: reporting every movement to the supplier will ensure that their records of what is at the customer warehouse are up to date, thus reducing the risk of stock-outs, but doing so has a cost. If a delivery of twenty pallets is received one pallet at a time, that is a lot of extra transactions and any cost savings projected by a move to consignment stock will soon be eaten up. True: consignment stock reduces the risk of stock-outs, but also taking costs out of the supply chain, as happened in the first example, has to be a better option for everyone than merely shuffling them around.

4.11 Safety or buffer stock

4.11.1 Why do I need it?

Safety stock is there to guard us against uncertainty. It is an admission that we can never be in total control. Some companies can control their customers and some their suppliers but none can do both (I suppose that you could say that government agencies come close but it is a moot point). The uncertainties that we face include, but are not limited to, the following:

- Variation in customer demand. We can forecast as much as we want, we can have the cleverest algorithms and software, the most accurate finger on the pulse but, when push comes to shove, we can't force our customers to buy what we what them to buy. Encourage, yes; force, no.
- Supplier uncertainty. We can agree delivery dates with our suppliers but unless we, as a customer, are of critical importance to them, we can't be totally confident that they will keep to those promises. Even then we can have problems when our supplier does not directly control the method of delivery: they may get the product to the factory door on time but can they control the haulier, the shipper and the customs authorities?
- Quality. We can carefully choose our suppliers; we can vet them and audit them regularly and, if we are big enough, we can even fine them if they let us down. But, in the best supply chains, with the best management and people, Murphy will always sooner or later score a point.

Let's have a look at these areas in a bit more detail and consider whether or not safety stock can help and, if it can, at which level of the bill of material should it be held and how much?

Variation in customer demand

Forecasting customer demand is one of the biggest challenges that we face. Demand for a product can go through the roof overnight if, for example, a product gets a favourable mention on television. Many a company has seen demand for a product take off vertically when a 'celebrity chef' uses it on a cookery programme. Others will experience an overnight increase in market share when a competitor goes bust. Either way; turning away business is rarely something that we wish to do.

One problem with forecasting is that it is frequently done at the wrong level of the bill of material. We will consider later whether forecasting should be done at the Master Production Schedule level (or whether Master Production Scheduling should be done at the forecast level) but for now we will just consider The Law of Big Numbers. Amongst other things, this law say that big numbers are easier to estimate.

How is that so? Well; if I was selling tins of baked beans, I might sell one million tins a week. If I was selling laptop computers, I might sell twenty thousand a week. In either case, the loss of one order is probably not going to break me (suppliers to Wal-Mart; look away now). On the other hand, I have worked with an outfit that budgets for sales of four units per year (they make radio stations). In their case, losing one order or gaining one order says that their sales forecast was 25% out. To some extent they are buffeted by a sales process that takes months so they generally (but not always) get a confidence in that forecast far enough out to prepare accordingly.

Many companies in the middle, though, are literally caught in the middle. They rely on forecasts and forecast inaccuracy hurts. Now let's be realistic: not many companies can forecast accurately at a product level (baked beans maybe; radio stations not). It is not through lack of trying, nor lack intelligence; it is just that we can't always control the scenarios that influence our customer's decisions. If our forecast is based on a customer getting a particular contract; what happens if they don't get it? If we are selling ice cream, what happens if summer starts early or finishes late? And, as we said before, what happens if a 'celebrity chef' mentions your product on prime time television? Trust me: these things are out of your control and cannot be forecast.

A good MRPII system helps us to implement The Law of Big Numbers by forecasting and planning at a product family level, where wild swings can sometimes be more comfortably accommodated. We looked at this in section 4.7.

Supplier uncertainty

As we said previously; whatever we do, our suppliers will, at some point, let us down however hard they try not to. It may be that they, in turn, have been let down by one of their suppliers or they might have had a critical machine breakdown: in fact, any of the things that happen to us could well happen to them also. So how to I reduce the chance of something going wrong in someone else's factory? I can't but I can lessen the impact that it has on me.

Firstly, I can make myself more important to my suppliers. I am not a believer in putting all of my eggs in one basket but I am a believer in limiting the number of suppliers that I use. My preference is to have, wherever possible, two suppliers for everything that I buy, and to split the business between them on a 70/30 basis. Minimising the number of my suppliers maximises my spend with them and makes me more important to them so that, when they have problems and can't deliver all of their orders, my orders are more likely to go to the front of the queue.

Why the 70/30 split, though? A split means that, not only do I have a second supplier already geared up to supply me if a problem occurs, but the 30% supplier knows that, if they perform well, they have a chance of doubling the amount of business that I do with them, and the 70% supplier knows that someone else can take a big chunk of their business if I have reason to be unhappy. Do I tell each of the suppliers about each other? I certainly do. Nothing commercial or confidential, of course, but if my business is important to them, they probably know of each other's existence anyway, and it does no harm to remind them occasionally that they have competition.

Some companies that I have worked with don't agree with me on this so let me tell you about two companies that I worked with. They are not only within a few miles of each other but they are of very similar size, are in the same market and make similar products. Not surprisingly then, they share not only customers but some suppliers also. One employs a buyer and does pretty much what I have been advising, whilst the other employs a purchasing manager, three buyers and three junior buyers.

Why the extra staff? Well; they believe they get better prices by going to tender on just about every order that they place, so they request, receive and compare quotes continually. Because they were both implementing new systems at the same time, I had access to their data and could make some comparisons. Granted, I could only compare a random selection of items but, on all of the comparisons that I made, bar none, the company that went to quote for everything was paying higher prices than the one that didn't, even when the supplier was the same.

Did I tell them about their competitor? Of course not: that would have been unethical and a betrayal of commercial confidence. But, without being specific, I did tell them that other companies in their industry were taking my advice and were benefitting from it. Sadly, they decided to stick to 'tried and tested' methodologies. (I can't give you a reference to follow up as they went bust a while back.)

How else can you minimise supplier uncertainty? Well, you can give your suppliers more information. If you have sales forecasts, you can extrapolate these into purchasing forecasts. I'm not suggesting that you should place purchase orders as far out as your sales forecasts go but I can't think of a good reason not to advise your suppliers of your intent to place orders with them in the future, as long as you make it clear to them that these are forecasts only and not firm commitments. Not only will you help them with their own plans but, by being seen to be trying to help, you may be seen to be a 'good guy' and that might get you preferential treatment when there are problems. (One of the advantages of minimising the number of people that you buy from is that you can afford to spend more time with them and begin to move from a customer/supplier relationship to a trading partner relationship.)

Quality

Sometimes quality has to be 'designed in' to a product and this concept is clearly beyond the scope of this book. Likewise, it is generally safer for your designers to use industry-standard items rather than have them bespoked for you. Not only can they be more reliable but, if something does go wrong, you may be able to get replacements faster.

What you can do is to talk to your suppliers (again easier if you have fewer of them and are more important to them). Some of these people really know and understand their products and, if they know what you are using them for, can be a source of good advice, whether on how to use a particular product better or, indeed, on whether there is an alternative product that could and should be used instead. Suppliers that I have had good relationships with have occasionally pointed me at products that were not only better for my purpose but cheaper too.

Naturally, when you do have a problem with their products, you should make time to discuss it with them (both the problem itself and the effect that it has had). I am not advocating that you beat up your suppliers but that, in complaining, you explain why you are complaining so that it is not just seen as a gripe. Inherent in this philosophy is that you should talk to your suppliers when you have problems and not just immediately ditch them and move on.

4.11.2 How much should I have?

And now the million dollar question: "How much safety stock do I need?". To that, I am going to add, "At what level of the bill of material should I have it?".

There are three places that you can hold safety stock: finished goods, sub-assemblies and raw materials. Your sales people will want you to have the maximum possible stock at the finished goods level so that they can maximise sales on an ex-stock basis. If you are selling in a market that demands ex-stock delivery, and you have long manufacturing lead times, you may be forced into that. However, there are two problems with this approach:

- It can cost a fortune
- You run a greater risk of high write-off or obsolescence costs if the market suddenly dies.

To which I should probably add a third: enough is never enough. There are algorithms out there that you can use to calculate the level of stock required to produce a given level of probability of stock availability but, as the probability rises, the costs of stock holding rise exponentially. If you can, in your mind's eye, look at your safety stock of finished goods and see all of the components or ingredients that make up those items, you will frequently find that, overall, you have the components that you need to satisfy orders but they have been built into the wrong products. That says that we should, wherever possible, be holding safety stock at a lower level in the bill of material and not at the finished item level.

If you are in a process industry, then your only other choice may be to hold your safety stock at the raw material level. Doing so will definitely give you the greatest flexibility and will minimise costs but there is a price to pay. If you have long manufacturing lead times, then even if you push shortage orders to the front of the queue and accept the costs of doing that (overtime, extra shifts, increased number of machine set-ups, potential risks to on-time delivery of other jobs etc), you may still end up with a delivery lead time that is unacceptable to the customer.

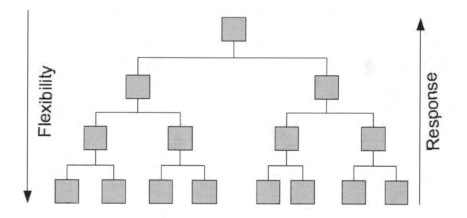

So somewhere we have to have a compromise; a balance between flexibility, costs and lead times. That point is going to be somewhere between raw materials and finished goods: one of the sub-assembly levels. But if you have multiple levels of sub-assembly, which should you choose? Let me tell you about a company that I worked with that made, amongst other items, wardrobes.

Their designers were switched on. They knew that, when they designed a carcase (comprising the top, bottom, sides and back), that same carcase could be made in a variety of finishes, such as pine, oak, sapele etc. They also knew that a new design could be created just by changing the style of door. Each finish of wardrobe carcase could then have multiple styles of door, and each door could be used on multiple carcases. From a relatively small number of carcase and door types, they could have a very large number of permutations (i.e. product types). The answer, then, was to hold stock of carcases and doors separately and assemble to order (ATO) as customer orders came in. That final assembly operation took minutes and made next-day despatch frequently possible.

A very similar approach was taken by a manufacturer of PCs and laptop computers that I worked with. They maintain stocks of sub-assemblies (memory boards, disc drives etc) and merely assemble them as orders come in: maximum flexibility, minimum lead times. Incidentally, they took the basic idea but then went one step further—they applied it to labour! They have a core of full-time assembly workers and a number of fully-trained, part-time workers who don't want to work every day but are happy to come in for a few days when demand is high.

Now; the stocks that I am talking about here cannot really be called safety stock. They are really designed to reduce manufacturing lead times so, in fact, have to have safety stocks themselves. So the question is; how much? Two things work in our favour here: the Law of Big Numbers, because we are dealing with items that are standard sub-assemblies and are consequently used across a range of end products, and the fact that, with such items, to some extent at least, we will be buffered against fluctuations in end product demand by 'swings and roundabouts'—an increase in demand for one end product may well be balanced by a decrease in demand for another. Actual demand can be surprisingly stable at this level.

There is no magic formula that we can use here. Pragmatically, it is usually better to start by looking through history and identifying the highest actual demand over a period—that period will be our replenishment lead time (see section 4.4 for a discussion on batch sizing), following which an iterative approach can be taken. We will quickly see a pattern of usage emerge and can adjust our stock levels accordingly.

4.11.3 At what level of the bill of material?

The remaining question to be answered is at what level in the bill of material this stock should be held at. If you make wardrobes or PCs, I may have already given you the answer but, if not, can we define a rule? Possibly so.

Let's start off by defining a term that I came across recently—'Point of divergence'. To understand it, let's look at the following representations of very simple bills.

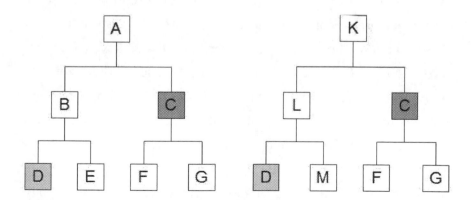

In these bills, end products A and K both share sub-assembly C. In our simple example, the components that go into C are unique to it.

However, this sub-assembly is not unique to its parents: both product A and product K use it. In these examples, sub-assembly C is a point of divergence: the point at which uniqueness ends. Component D is also a point of divergence, as it is used in both sub-assemblies B and L.

Perhaps un-naturally, because we have only two products, components E and N are unique and safety stock of those would have to be held also, as we shouldn't hold stock of sub-assemblies B or L lest we tie up item D un-necessarily. With safety stock held against sub-assembly C, we have removed the need for safety stock of F and G. If we break the rules and hold it there also, we will be duplicating our efforts; expensively and un-necessarily.

But there will be occasions when you need to have safety stock at a raw material level to cope with supplier and quality variability, as discussed earlier. How much, then, should you hold? That depends to a large extent on our supplier lead times. Let's take the worst-case scenario: you have just received a shipment from a supplier and it has failed inspection. How soon can the supplier send replacements? How much are you likely to need in the interim? Answers to those questions tell me how much safety stock you need. Obviously, if you have taken the two-supplier, 70/30 split discussed earlier, you have more options. Perhaps you have an existing order with the second supplier that can be increased and brought forward (remember the arguments for the 70/30 split? See section 4.11.1.)

Of course, not all companies can inspect every item and it can then be the case that a batch or delivery is not discovered to be unusable until problems show up on the production line. If you are in an industry where you get very regular deliveries (some of the companies that I work with get multiple deliveries of the same items every day) then things can be easier. If you have very regular deliveries and if they are likely to come from different supplier batches, it is frequently (though not always) the case that the problem is limited to one delivery. In which case the safety stock that you need to hold is one delivery's worth. If it is likely that the supplier makes multiple deliveries to me from one of his batches, then it is possible that all of his on-hand stock is suspect. In those circumstances, you would be advised to talk to your suppliers to find out how they operate *before* things go wrong.

4.12 Data Accuracy

Anyone who has been within a country mile of an MRP/MRPII installation knows that data accuracy is paramount but advice on how to achieve it is thin on the ground, so let's look at why we need it and what we can do to achieve it.

For MRP to work well, we need accuracy in the following areas:

- Bills of Material

    Are they complete and do they accurately reflect the way the product is actually made on the shop floor, as opposed to the way that the design office thinks that it is made?
- Stock static data

    Are manufacturing lead times accurate and, notwithstanding what we said about purchasing lead times in section 4.2, are these reasonable too? Are batch sizing rules correct?

- Stock balances

  Are your stock figures accurate and do they reflect usable stock only (i.e. excluding rejects, items that have passed their expiry dates etc)? And, if you use locations on your stock records, are these accurate too? If you don't know where stock is, you might as well not have it.

- Outstanding purchase orders

  Do these accurately reflect what is actually on order, in terms of quantity and due date? Are there old orders on the system, perhaps with trivial outstanding quantities, that everyone knows will never actually be delivered?

- Outstanding works orders (the above comments on purchase orders also apply here)

- Outstanding sales orders (the same rules apply).

Those are six things that we have to get right, but let's have fun for a moment and assume that, just for the sake of argument, we believe these areas to all be 90% accurate (insert your own figures or estimates later). So with each of these areas 90% accurate, MRP will be 90% accurate; right?

Well, actually; no.

It is (90% x 90% x 90% x 90% x 90% x 90%) / 6 = 53% accurate.

Putting that another way; almost half of the recommendations that MRP will produce will be inaccurate. Now, we can argue about just how inaccurate they are (perhaps a bill of material says we use two washers but the shop floor always use four; perhaps an old purchase order says that, of the 1,000 items that we ordered, only 990 were delivered so 10 remain on order) but we have to remember that little things add up and, over a period of time, can have a marked effect. A human being can look at an old purchase order and know that those ten items will never be delivered but a computer can't. If we tried to build in a rule, it would be clear that 10 washers, twelve months overdue are unlikely to be delivered, but what if it was 1,000 washers, one week overdue? Where would the cut-offs be, in terms of time and quantity? The only answer is to get our data right and to keep it right, so let's work through our list and look at what can be done.

4.12.1 Bills of Material

As with the other elements, we have two challenges: getting them right and keeping them right. The first challenge is getting new bills onto the system, remembering that they should be both accurate and complete (though see section 4.6 for handling incomplete bills). In companies where the design department is divorced from the production engineering department, several things can go wrong:

Design can list the important components but not bother to include items that they consider to be obvious or trivial. Why bother including the electric plug on the bill of material for a kettle? Everyone knows that it needs one, and the stores are full of them anyway. But the computer isn't 'everyone' and the reason that the stores are full of them is that someone told the system that they were needed. I have seen a £50,000 piece of equipment not despatched because no-one told the system about the eight bolts that were required to attach it to a skid.

Yes; remembering all of the apparently trivial components is a pain but some help, at least, is at hand. You will recall that, in section 3.7, when discussing phantom bills of material, we said that one use of phantoms was to cluster items into a 'virtual' sub-assembly. You might care to consider having phantom bills of material for all of the items that design consider to be trivial so that, e.g. a cable, plug, fuse etc can be added to the bill as one line item.

The next thing that you have to check is that production make the item as design intended. The first people to check with are the production engineering department, who have the skills and authority to amend designs to make products easier, cheaper and faster to produce. Are these amendments finding their way into the bill? Is there a formal system to facilitate this, or do you have to rely on people remembering?

Then you have to consider how the data is getting into the system. I have seen many instances of design and production engineering doing good jobs of getting the data together and then passing it to temps or clerks who don't understand what they are looking at; nor the importance of 100% accuracy. When a bill of material is entered to the system; how many of us print it out and have it checked and signed-off? Not enough of us, I would guess.

Getting bills of material onto the system accurately is only half of the problem. Many companies have intelligent people on their shop floors and these people frequently find better or easier ways of doing things. Unofficial design changes start to creep in: "Yes, I know we should be using the ABC123 but, if I use an XYZ456 with an extra washer, it's much easier to install and does exactly the same job". How many variations of that have we heard over the years?

Now; you don't want to stop advantageous design changes just because they come from the shop floor but what you do want to do is ensure that they get into the system and that they are agreed by all (does everyone use the XYZ456 with the extra washer or just those in the know?). So how do you identify these shop floor changes? Well, you may have mechanisms in place already. Not only Japanese companies have shopfloor and multi-disciplined teams continuously looking for improvements, and some companies that have not yet gone down that route have suggestion schemes in place. Whichever way you look at it, the information you need is generally there for the asking. (If you are a company whose employees are afraid to tell you that they are making such changes then you need more help than this book can offer.) Build the canal and the water will flow.

All of this helps you change the future but, if you are loading existing bills into a new system, how can you do a catch-up to ensure that they are accurate today. Many text books recommend that you do a test dis-assembly of a product: try telling that to someone who mixes chemicals or welds metal. Besides; how many products do you have? Hopefully, the new system hasn't just appeared overnight so you have other, more viable, options.

Even if you are not currently running an MRP system, you will have a record somewhere of what you believe goes into your products. In the months leading up to go-live, give a copy of this information to your teams on the shop floor and ask them to check-off what they actually use. Even if you have to guarantee them bonus payments that they might otherwise lose, the investment will pay for itself many times over. A sometimes interesting first pass on this method is the 'decibel test'—show the shopfloor your official bills of material and the louder they laugh, the more inaccurate you know they are! Trust me: if these people make an item regularly, they know better than you what goes into it. Tap into that knowledge.

Sometimes you can come at the problem from another angle; particularly if you are already using some kind of MRP system. If your bills of material are inaccurate, but products are still being made, then discrepancies may be showing up in your stocktakes. Components that are being used beyond the usage suggested by the bills will frequently show up as shortages, whilst those that are not being used will show up as excesses.

One last thing to consider on bill of material accuracy: we have been talking about the components and quantities that find their way into product but we haven't discussed the items that find their way into the scrap bin. If these quantities are significant (and having checked, you might find that they are more significant than you realise) then you have to decide how to deal with these. Much depends on how you issue components and replacement components. If you backflush and the scrap rate is reasonably consistent, one answer is to build the expected wastage into the bill of material. This has the added benefit of making a cost roll-up more representative of actual costs. If you are dealing with expensive items, these will frequently be under tighter control and people will be more aware of the importance of transacting replacements properly (the previous comments about companies operating with a fear culture that prevents people from being honest about scrap and waste most definitely still apply—I want people to give me bad news so that I can do something about it, not hide it so I can't).

4.12.2 Stock Static Data

We have already discussed the accuracy of manufacturing and purchasing lead times in sections 4.2 and 4.3. Other elements that are frequently wrong in computer systems are:

- batch sizing rules
- minimum or safety stocks
- inappropriate units of measure
- costs.

Most of these have, again, already been discussed, so we will not dwell on them here. Suffice to say that the introduction of a new system will be your best chance to get your data right until your *next* new system, and that should be years away. If you don't clean up your data now, you will end up limping along with it for a very long time.

One big thing that you should think about when cleaning up your data is how many duplicate part numbers you have. It sounds obvious to say that the more part numbers you have, the more duplicates you have. Apart from the scaling factor, large numbers of part numbers dissuade the people responsible for raising new ones from searching through hundreds or thousands of records to find if part numbers already exist: it is less work to just create new ones. This doesn't affect these people directly (apart from the fact that the files are again bigger the next time they search for a part; so they raise a new number again).

It does, however, frequently affect the company, and for several reasons:

- you may find that you are duplicating safety stocks unnecessarily by holding them against two, three or more part numbers.
- you may find that you are incurring extra costs by placing rush orders for items that you already have in stock.
- you may find that you are missing out on quantity discounts from suppliers.

Regardless: duplicating part numbers is bad practice.

Finding duplicates, however, can be difficult. One way is to print off your part numbers and item descriptions in description sequence but that only works if descriptions follow a very clear format and everyone calls items the same thing (is it cable or flex; a ball valve or a valve, ball?). If more than one person has been responsible for creating descriptions over the years, it is very difficult to maintain a discipline.

It can be more effective to sort by another field on the stock file. When considering purchased items, are we recording our supplies' part numbers on our stock file? If we are buying the same item under multiple part numbers, we probably are still paying the same price, so that might be another sort option.

4.12.3 Stock Balances

This is the one that really hurts. Having less stock than we think we have causes stock-outs which cause production stoppages which result in unhappy customers. Having more stock than we think we have means that we are tying up money and space unnecessarily. So what can we do? Let's consider why stock figures go wrong in the first place. Reasons include:

- Un-transacted replacement issues
- Un-transacted scrap and write-offs
- Unofficial use of alternatives
  ○ Human error
  ○ Under or over transacting
- Under or over issuing
- If we are backflushing, inaccurate bills of material.

Note that I haven't listed an open stores policy as a reason. That is because such a policy is an excuse for inaccurate stocks; not a reason. I have worked with companies that operate open stores yet have almost perfect stock accuracy because systems are in place to capture withdrawals and they have taken the time to educate their staff. A good way to start this education is to say to your people, "Isn't it frustrating when you go to a shelf for an item and it isn't there?" I have never known anyone say "No". Then point out that the reason it wasn't there is that no-one had bothered to tell the system that someone had taken the ones that were there previously. Most people don't deliberately do a bad job: it's just that they are not always told what a good job is.

It goes without saying, I hope, that a new system should start off with an accurate stock check and not just a transfer of balances from the old system. If you start off with accurate stocks, how can you ensure that they stay accurate?

First, having checked all of your bills of material, you should put in place the measures already discussed in section 4.12.1 to ensure that they stay accurate. This is vital for MRP to work properly and, if you are backflushing inaccurate bills of material, the damage is obvious.

You also need to ensure that you have procedures and policies in place to ensure that all stock movements are reported to the system and that everyone understands the importance of this. These policies and procedures will also cover the issue of replacements when the originals have been lost or damaged so it is imperative that you have a culture that allows people to be honest when something goes wrong. If you criticise or punish people who are being honest, you can be sure that they will find ways around any procedures that you put in place.

The unreported use of alternatives is most apparent in the despatch process. It is not unusual for despatch staff to be authorised to use alternatives if allocated stock can't be found, especially if despatch is taking place out of hours. Sometimes the stock is actually there, but not in the location expected and, under pressure of time, pragmatic decisions are taken. This is fine as far as it goes but the damage occurs when the substitution is not reported to the system. At some point in the future, the system allocates the stock that was sent out as substitute and the cycle continues. Very soon, everyone in despatch knows that the data in the official stock system is inaccurate but they forget why. Incidentally, this scenario was a major cause of the three separate stock systems in one company, mentioned in section 2. The key, then, is to ensure that the system makes it easy to allow substitutions to be recorded and transacted. If the importance of doing so is then transmitted to the despatch staff, the result will be less hassle for everyone—including those same despatch staff!

Whilst mentioning that stock is sometimes there but just not exactly where we think it is, a short discussion on stock location systems is warranted. I have seen stores and warehouses where everything is located in reserved locations, sometimes even in part number sequence. If you can do this, it is a perfect solution but, for most companies, circumstances mitigate against it:

- space is expensive and, unless your stock levels remain relatively constant (and that is rare), you will find yourself tying up space that could be better utilised
- if you store in part number sequence, what happens when you introduce new part numbers? Consecutive part numbers do not always take up the same amount of space so some items might fit easily into trays whilst others take up whole pallet positions.

If you can justify it and afford it, a full-blown warehousing system, complete with bar coding and put-away instructions, is ideal but it is a major investment for most manufacturing companies who traditionally find it easier to spend money on sexier projects. So what generally happens is that stores and warehouse staff have to make the most of what space they have. We have all seen deliveries shunted into aisles or other temporary locations and we have all seen staff shuffling stock around to make room.

Most MRPII systems offer location control in their stock control module, enabling stock to be pin-pointed to a particular warehouse, aisle, rack, location and tray. The benefits are enormous, as pick lists can show this information and point the stock picker at the exact location where the allocated stock is to be found. This works great. Until staff have to shunt stock around. At that stage, if the relocation cannot be reported to the system quickly and easily, it won't be. People may well start off with good intentions; determined to bring the system up-to-date when they get time but, sooner or later, things get forgotten and scribbled notes get lost.

What happens then is that location control becomes inaccurate and the pick lists no longer show valid locations for the items required. That sends the system into a downward spiral: if locations are wrong, they are not worth updating. If they don't get updated, they get more wrong and the system falls into disrepute (and spreadsheet stock control systems start to appear outside of the formal system).

Remember that, if we don't know where our stock is, the result is exactly the same as not having that stock in the first place. We need, therefore, to strike a balance between finite accuracy as to where the stock is located, and the amount of effort (and as a result, the reducing probability) involved in keeping those location records current. It can be more pragmatic, and more beneficial in the long run, to go for greater granularity with locations: recording the aisle that items are in may be more practical than getting down to bins and trays, however much this might offend and disappoint us. Of course, there is no reason why we can't set ourselves targets to improve matters and some items may be less troublesome than others and lend themselves to that tighter control from Day One. In this area, one size rarely fits all.

4.12.4 Residue Purchase Orders

For MRP to give accurate purchase recommendations, it has to know what is on order and when it is due for delivery. Two things frequently go wrong. One is that purchase orders, particularly in some industries, are frequently short delivered and the quantities involved can be trivial. If you have been short delivered expensive items, you can probably expect delivery of the balance. But, if the items are not expensive and relatively small quantities are involved, your suppliers are likely to call the order complete rather than incur the administration and transport costs involved in delivering a trivial balance. Indeed, in some industries such as packing materials, a delivery quantity tolerance is the norm.

Now; we rarely mind if we are short delivered 50 items against an order quantity of 1,000. But, if items are ordered regularly, it doesn't take long for the false picture of 50 on order to become a false picture of hundreds on order and for MRP to believe that a new order is unnecessary. True; the system will generate reports saying that these residue quantities are outstanding and overdue, but if you don't have the discipline to clear them down, you probably don't have the discipline to react to trivial quantities on these reports either. As we said before, a human being can look at an outstanding quantity on an order and make an assumption as to its validity but a computer can't.

So what do we do about these residue quantities? Some systems have receiving options that, if not eliminating the problem, at least minimise it. The most frequent of these is the ability to specify a tolerance on the system such that a receipt percentage that crosses this threshold automatically closes the order unless manually overridden.

The advantage of this is that, for the majority of cases, no manual intervention is required. The disadvantage is that, if the threshold percentage is held at a system level, it has to be a compromise: if I am ordering packaging, I might be happy to set it at, say, 95% but for other items I might need and demand 100% of what I ordered. Nevertheless, it is a very good place to start, especially if the system allows orders to be re-opened to cope with instances when the residue is unexpectedly delivered.

The other option, and perhaps only option if you don't have the functionality mentioned above, is to use a reporting tool to display daily or weekly receipts and residue quantities and then to close-out orders manually. However, this requires more user intervention and, particularly during busy periods, disciplines tend to slip. It is generally better to adopt the first approach and deal with exceptions manually.

The other important item of data on a purchase is the expected delivery date. When we first raise an order, this will be our required delivery date unless we have previously contacted the supplier to agree an alternative date. When the supplier receives the order, it is likely that they will make a decision on the viability of that date and, if they cannot make it, we can expect them to send us an order acknowledgement with an alternative delivery specified. Some suppliers will, of course, just take the order regardless of whether they can deliver on-time or not but we should be filtering these people out of our supplier list as we need suppliers that we can depend on.

Whether we receive a revised delivery date when the order is placed, or receive it as a consequence of subsequent expediting, it is imperative that the new delivery date gets onto the system so that the rest of the plan can make sense. If the items can't be delivered on time, and we can't arrange alternatives, we need to change the production plan so that our customer doesn't get an unwelcome surprise and so that other items that are required on the job, and which may be expensive or have limited shelf lives, can be rescheduled in line with new expectations.

All of this involves the giving of bad news, and no-one enjoys being such a messenger. Our supplier's sales office probably doesn't want to tell us that they can't deliver on time (especially if they think that by doing so they will lose the order). Our buyers won't want to tell our production people lest it reflect badly on their ability as buyers. Our production people won't want to tell our sales people because they fear criticism at the next inter-departmental meeting (and something might miraculously happen in the meantime) and our sales people won't want to tell the customer because they fear losing new orders (and the customer might just not notice that the order was delivered late).

But, as an ex-buyer and ex-production manager, I don't want people to hide bad news from me (remember that your customer is generally a buyer also). If you give me bad news early enough, I have a chance to plan around the problem or to arrange alternatives. If I can do so, then even though you have let me down, I am much more likely to continue doing business with you than I would be if the first I hear of your problem is when my expected delivery doesn't arrive. When that happens, you will cause me extra expense by having to react urgently and you will cause me to disappoint my customers; jeopardising my relationships with them. You will have lost my trust and I will actively look for an alternative supplier. Give me the bad news up front and you reduce not only my costs but also the amount of hassle that I personally am going to get. Which of these two suppliers stands the better chance of getting my repeat business? That is a 'No brainer'.

One last thought: false purchase orders (and works and sales orders, for that matter) not only impact on MRP's accuracy but also on its run time.

4.12.5 Residue Works Orders

Much of what was said above about purchase orders holds true for works orders also. They have to reflect what is actually expected to happen and not just represent a wish or a hope. The expected manufacturing dates must be kept in line with reality because they will have both upstream and downstream effects. On the one hand, they will affect purchasing activity and such items will come in too early or too late if the system is not informed and plans amended accordingly. On the other; they will result in our customers feeling as let down as we feel when our suppliers don't pre-warn us of late deliveries. We also invalidate our capacity plans and schedules.

Some industries have the problem of knowing whether residue quantities on works orders will be completed or not. Leaving orders open when they should be closed ties up stock in un-necessary and false component allocations; potentially triggering unnecessary replenishment orders. There are various reasons why works orders are not always completed when they should be but they generally revolve around problems of communication; particularly when the completions are not done by the shopfloor but by warehouse staff.

The problem is worse when multiple part-completions of works orders are the norm (for example, when items are booked into stock by the warehouse, they may do a part-completion on the arrival of each pallet load).

We don't want to delay stock bookings, especially when this can delay despatches, but how do we tell the warehouse that production against a particular works order has ended? Sometimes we are tempted to look for sophisticated answers to problems but, in this instance, the solution can be simple and cheap. Get yourselves some large, bright, sticky labels and give them to the shopfloor. In the vast majority of cases they know when they have finished (an exception would be when they expect some component shortages to be made good, not knowing that they won't be). All they have to do is to attach one of these labels to the last pallet or pack produced. As mentioned, there will be exceptions but deal with exceptions exceptionally. A good system can cope with exceptions but is not built around them.

One last thought: putting in a computer system does not preclude people from talking to each other. Perhaps production control, the shopfloor and the warehouse people need a five minute meeting every day just to clear up queries. Don't, whatever you do, formalise these by having them in a conference room with coffee on tap. You will wait fifteen minutes for the inevitable stragglers to drift in and then everyone will settle down for detailed conversation and debate; comfortable in the belief that their lack of activity is justified because they are 'in a meeting'. Make such meetings (and many other meetings) 'stand up' meetings. The rule of such meetings is that no-one can sit down—you will be surprised how much shorter meetings become!

4.12.6 Residue Sales Orders

Again; many of the things already said about purchase orders and works order apply. Shortfalls on sales order despatches fall into two categories:

- those known about before despatch was triggered, and
- those which only become apparent at the point of despatch.

There will be occasions when we knowingly will short-deliver against a sales order. If we are selling from stock, we may know up front that we do not have the full quantity in stock and may have agreed with the customer that the residue is inconsequential. Some systems will allow the person triggering the despatch to close the order short but a less favourable way may be required, such as altering the order quantity to match the quantity available. I called this 'less favourable' because it denies visibility of the shortfall in subsequent reports. If you don't have visibility of shortfalls, you may feel that everything is going fine even though you are irritating your customers. Nevertheless, you are making a conscious decision to short-deliver and can close off the order accordingly. There will be occasions when the person who is triggering the despatch doesn't know whether the residue is still en route. A radical proposal there is that people should actually talk to each other: the invention of computers didn't make telephones obsolete!

The second type of shortfall occurs when the person triggering the despatch believes there to be sufficient stock available and the problem is not discovered until the point of despatch. It may be that the stocks were inaccurate (see section 4.12.3) or that a problem occurred at the point of despatch. Perhaps some items were found to be damaged or perhaps there just wasn't room for the full quantity on the delivery vehicle. These problems may well occur out of office hours and you will doubtless have procedures for coping with them. Some systems will allow amended despatch documents to be created whilst other will necessitate that the original documents be hand-annotated. The important thing is that your procedures should state clearly who is responsible for deciding whether the shortfall needs to be re-scheduled and who is responsible for updating the system with whatever decision has been taken.

Two last thoughts on data accuracy: do you have systems in place to measure it regularly and do you have teams in place to continually look at improving it?

5. The selection process

As we mentioned in a previous chapter, early MRP systems developed into MRPII systems and then into ERP systems as more and more functional areas were incorporated into the system. This happened to such an extent that ERP systems are now used increasingly by non-manufacturing companies by the simple expedient of using only the financial and commercial elements of the system and ignoring the rest. Utilities companies, insurance companies, hospitals and a host of others still need to buy, sell and account for their activities. They also need all, or most, of the things that were wrapped around MRPII to turn it into ERP, such as CRM (Customer Relationship Management), payroll, personnel management and a host of other modules.

This book, though, deals only with MRP and MRPII because that is where the author's knowledge and experience lies and because these are at the core of all manufacturing ERP systems. If you are a manufacturing organisation, they are the bits that you absolutely have to get right. If you are not a manufacturing organisation, on the other hand, this book is not for you. Although it contains information on topics such as system selection and system implementation that are of interest to all organisations, you would be better advised to buy a book that is aimed at your area specifically. Likewise there are enough books on CRM and accounting for those areas, important or vital though they be, to be largely ignored here.

The first question for a manufacturing company that is looking at MRP/MRPII systems is whether they should be. Not all manufacturing companies can or should use a system that has come from an MRP background. MRP was developed by and for manufacturing companies that make the same products repetitively and have materials scheduling and supply problems. So let's look at the types of company that probably shouldn't be using it.

Some manufacturing activity is carried out in companies that are generically called 'job shops'. MRP is largely an irrelevance for these companies for a number of reasons, including:

- Every job is a customer specific one-off, with very little repeatability. Only the most commonly used materials will be held in stock and, instead of a structured bill of materials, a parts list generally suffices because manufacturing lead times tend to be short. Some MRPII systems allow a one-off bill of material to be constructed at a works order level but it is not usually worthwhile to spend time creating a multi-level bill of material that will never be used again, even if a 'copy and amend' feature is available.
- Materials (with the exception of frequently used items and consumables) will be bought for specific jobs. The ability of MRP to consolidate demand is unnecessary and perhaps confusing, particularly as job shops tend to have very short order books and fast order turn over.
- Cost estimating will have had a very big part to play before getting the order and, as estimating systems vary greatly from industry to industry, only very limited functionality in this area is built into commercial MRPII systems. Furthermore,

because all jobs are one-offs against a pre-agreed price based on an estimate, there is rarely an advantage to creating a routing for work in progress and labour or machine usage tracking. True: many MRPII systems have job costing or project accounting modules that address these areas for companies that have complex requirements that cannot be met by job shop systems, which tend to be simpler and lack a lot of the commercial functionality inherent in MRPII, but for true job shops there is generally too much functionality in MRPII and that unnecessary functionality comes at a cost.

Leading on from that last point takes us to project manufacturing. These companies deal with products and order sizes and values on a much bigger scale than job shops. Examples would be the manufacture of specialist vehicles or capital plant. It is not that MRP and MRPII can't work successfully in such environments: they can and they do. However, the many companies that have successfully implemented MRP/MRPII in such companies have had to learn new ways of thinking. Consider the following three statements:

- I only want to consider requirements for job 1234.
- I need to know if everything for job 1234 has been ordered.
- I need to know if everything for job 1234 has been delivered.

These statements are at odds with the very philosophy of MRP and, if similar statements are voiced daily in your organisation, then you should not go down the MRP/MRPII route. Trust me: you will spend a lot of money and never be satisfied.

The remainder of this chapter deals with the selection of a suitable software package. For some companies this just means selecting a 'big name'—after all, 50 million lemmings can't all be wrong; can they? It is true that there are few bad solutions on the market today but every package, big or small, has its strengths and weaknesses and, if you are about to stake your reputation on a package, don't you owe it to the company and to yourself to check what you are getting into?

5.1 Launching the project

The first thing to stress is that selection of a new system is a team game in which every department that will be using the system must participate. There will be departments that consider themselves too busy to get involved, especially if they don't feel confident in their ability to contribute. Frequently, one particular department will be behind the drive for a new system and other departments will be happy to devolve responsibility for selection to anyone willing to do the work. We will have a look later at the dangers of allowing this but, at this stage, let's just point out three:

- Departments that devolve responsibility for this phase will want to devolve responsibility for the implementation phase also.
- That, in turn, means that they will feel no sense of ownership for the final system.
- One consequence of this is that, at times when maximum effort is required from everyone to get the system up and running, these people will feel free to look away and let it fail.

Ironically, having handed over responsibility for selection and implementation, these same people later may want a right of veto on the selection and perhaps even the implementation of the system. The minimum damage that this can do is that the selection process will have to be repeated, and perhaps repeated again and again, until the departments that exclude themselves from the process pronounce themselves happy with the choice (they never will be). Even worse is when the veto is applied after the system has been purchased. In these circumstances, the system never goes live or, at best, goes live in only some areas with perhaps some other departments paying lip service to it whilst returning to their 'tried and tested' spreadsheets. This area is so important that we will come back to it in the chapter 'What goes wrong?'.

One more problem that you need to consider, even before the selection phase begins, is that all package software is a compromise. All systems on the market have different strengths and weaknesses and those strengths and weaknesses will affect departments in different ways, making a particular package less suitable for some areas than others. For example, some packages come from a finance background and later have manufacturing modules added; whilst some are very strong in manufacturing areas but have third-party financial modules. During the selection phase, each member of the team will, not surprisingly, have their own department's requirements foremost in their mind and consequently, when it comes for a choice to be made, the decision is rarely unanimous.

However you choose between the systems evaluated, there will then be individuals on the team that feel they have lost out in the selection process. When their home departments see the chosen system, they may be disappointed that hoped-for and requested functionality and features are not to be delivered. What can happen then is that those individuals and departments will actively campaign against the new system in the hope that they can get the decision overturned. They will put every obstacle that they can think of in the way of the implementation and spend more time than the company can afford on thinking of reasons why the new system cannot work.

The amount of effort that these people will put into undermining the implementation team cannot be over-estimated. The lack of enthusiasm that they portray will affect whole departments, who will then believe that the company has made a bad choice and selected a system that will not only fail to meet their department's needs but will actually make things worse. Even if implemented, the system is on a fast track to failure as people find ways and excuses not to use it. Enter departmental systems and spreadsheets again. We will look at this again in the 'What can go wrong' chapter.

Getting back to the project, the first thing that you will need to do is get a structure in place. You will need a selection team, which will later become your core implementation team, a project manager and a project sponsor at the very highest level of management.

5.2 The Selection Team

The team needs to have a representative from each department that will be involved in the system, including the IT department. It is also a good idea to have in the team respected members of departments that will not be involved with the system. These people, not having any particular axe to grind, can be useful sounding boards and arbiters. They can be very useful in asking questions that everyone *thinks* they know the answer to and therefore don't ask, and they can also add value by occasionally pointing out that the Emperor has no clothes on. Their impartiality also makes them good candidates for the project manager role.

Mistakes are frequently made in the selection of people to make up the team. It is natural that heads of departments will want to represent their own areas, and in smaller companies there might be no other option, but in medium and larger companies it is generally not a good idea. The amount of time that will be required, even at the selection stage, is such that managers soon have to make choices between allocating time to the project and to their regular responsibilities. One area will suffer and it will generally be the project, as this will appear less urgent. When this happens, the project will be passed to a deputy but changing horses in mid-stream is rarely a good idea. So let's look at the alternatives.

One choice would be a promising young member of the department, on the grounds that involvement in the project will be a useful contribution to their career development. This can work really well, as such people can be very enthusiastic and energetic, but it is absolutely essential that the people who will be representing their departments have the confidence and respect of the people that they will be representing. If a young and up-coming member of staff has that confidence and respect, they will be a good choice but, if not, they can find themselves exposed, lose confidence and retreat from the task.

The best option is to give the task to your best and most indispensable person; the corollary of that, of course, is that you should never give it to your most dispensable person; the person that you can most easily spare. In a small company, on a small implementation, when you second your best person to the project, you will be taking up probably half of their time for, at the very least, three months. In a larger company and on a larger implementation, you will be taking your best person out of the front line, full time, for up to a year or more.

It is very easy to understand heads of department not wanting to do that but that is exactly what they must do if the project is to be a success. If you can't afford to put your best people on a task that could seriously damage the company if not performed successfully, then stop the project now. A second rate implementation is a waste of everyone's time and energy, to say nothing of the company's money. A project that is postponed can be re-started at some point in the future but I know from experience that a failed implementation is very, very difficult to turn around. It can be done, but it costs twice as much as it would have cost had it been done properly in the first place and there will be casualties along the way. Don't risk your reputation and your job by going down this route.

I shouldn't have to point out the dangers of giving the task to your most dispensable person but I will. Sometimes we have people who are working out their notice period, or drifting to retirement. Sometimes we have people who really are not up to the jobs they have but, for whatever reason, we can't fire them so the temptation is to pull them out of the front line and put them in a task which seems less mission-critical. To understand why you need your best people on the team, let's look at and understand the task they will be performing.

The task of the team is firstly to articulate the requirements of each department in a document that competing systems will be measured against, frequently called an Invitation to Tender (ITT) or Statement of User Requirements (SOUR). They will need to understand the difference between wants and needs; between essential and nice to have. They will emphatically not just be documenting the current system but will be actively engaged in thinking about how the company should be operating in the future. At the risk of being accused of playing with the Queen's English; they must be able to differentiate between what you are trying to do and what you are trying to achieve. They must understand how their departments work and what is important to those departments. Later in the selection process, they must have the maturity and intellect to work as a respected member of a team that will be assessing and evaluating alternatives. If representatives do not have the respect of their peers in the selection team, they will be marginalised and their department's voice in the process will not be heard.

One thing that gets inadequate attention, when putting together a team like this, is that all team members should, if at all possible, be of equal standing in the company. To understand why this should be so, consider the following two possibilities that have, admittedly, been exaggerated in order to make very clear points.

- In the first scenario, the team is made up of a manager and a number of senior clerical staff. Who do you think will have a disproportionate say in any decisions taken?

- Turning that around; imagine a team of several managers and one senior clerk. How much influence do you think that clerk is going to have in any decisions taken?

As a departmental manager, you may think that you can post a second rate staff member to the team and, by micro-managing them and by demanding a right of veto, control the situation. Believe me; you won't. You will spend so much time checking on them, their actions and decisions, that you will rapidly conclude that you need to be involved full time, and we have already established that, in all but the smallest companies and implementations, this is not viable.

5.3 Project Manager Selection

Having considered the structure of the team, we now need to consider the role of the project manager. As mentioned before, a respected member of a department not involved in the project can be a very good choice; particularly if they come from a department where projects are common, thus having project management skills and experience already. These can be your IT or Engineering departments, for example. Most important is that the project manager should be, and be recognised as being, independent of any inter-departmental politics and not in favour any particular department.

That leads some companies to employ an external consultant as project manager, with the added advantage that consultants can have experience of having led multiple selections and implementations in the past. It is, without doubt, imperative to have system selection and implementation experience on the team. No sane person goes on a journey for the first time without a guide or a detailed road map provided by such a guide, but how independent are consultants?

If you hire a consultant from one of the major consultancies, be aware that many of these have relationships with JBOPS (the acronym for JD Edwards, Baan, Oracle, PeopleSoft and SAP; the heavyweights in the ERP/MRPII market). These systems take hundreds, and sometimes thousands, of days of consultancy support to implement and, to meet this demand, the big consultancies have set up and trained teams of the necessary people. Your problem is that, if you choose consultants to lead your selection, and they have expensive teams that are currently under-utilised, how impartial do you think their advice can be? They will be under enormous internal pressure to use their own resource and will also feel happier working with software that they know rather than venture into the unknown. That will lead them to recommend the system that is best for **them** but not necessarily best for you.

So what of independent consultants? Again we have to ask ourselves how truly independent they are. Many small consultancies have relationships with the smaller software suppliers; working on a reciprocity basis and recommending each other to their clients. As with the large consultancies, they will not only be more comfortable with software that they have experience of but will know that their value in the implementation phase will be enhanced if they know the system selected; thus improving their chances of follow-on work. So how do you find where consultants' primary loyalty lies? Well, hopefully, you already have relationships with consultants and, having asked them, you know them well enough to know when they are being evasive (or worse).

The other thing that you can do is to use your contacts. You have customers, suppliers and a host of people that you have access to via professional bodies. What software do they use, what consultants aided them in the selection and implementation phases and what would they do differently the next time around? (Note that people don't always want to admit that they did something wrong or that they made bad decisions, but feel easier in listing what they learnt—which frequently points to the same thing.) There really is an awful lot of information out there if you just take the time and trouble to link in to it. One last thing that you can do, if working with new consultants, is to ask for CVs of the people they will be sending in, along with brief details of their last ten or twelve jobs. If you see that a disproportionate number of those were implementing a particular software package, you might want to ask why.

If you do decide to bring in an external consultant as a project manager because you lack experience within the company of project management, I would urge that their remit explicitly excludes a role in system selection. They should tell you how to set selection criteria but they should not be part of setting those criteria. They should tell you how to pick a shortlist but they should not be part of picking it. They should tell you how to evaluate software against your needs but they should not evaluate it.

They do, however, have an important role to play during software demonstrations. I am sure that you will not be shocked to hear that not all software suppliers are ethical and not all salesmen are scrupulously honest. The clever ones will not actually tell lies but they will allow themselves to be misunderstood and, when telling the truth, they will not necessarily tell *all* it (to use an infamous phrase from British politics, they will be 'economical with the truth'). An experienced consultant should be able to spot this and to ask for clarification when necessary. The world is full of people who didn't buy what they thought they were buying.

One last thought on the selection of a project manager. If you do not have project management skills in-house and you do not want to, or cannot afford to, hire an external consultant, you are left with handing the role to someone who meets all of the other criteria but lacks these vital skills. No-one can become a good project manager overnight but you can at least send them on a brief project management course without breaking the bank. They will not come back fully-skilled (that takes years of study and experience; as does any similar skill) but you will at least have reduced the risk of project management failure and given them a chance of doing a half-decent job.

5.4 Project Management Role

Responsibilities of the project manager during the selection phase are as follows (we will look at their responsibilities during the implementation phase later).

- Setting deadlines and arranging and leading meetings to monitor progress with the production of the ITT/SOUR.
- Monitoring team member performance and their attendance at project meetings and reporting problems to the project sponsor.
- Acting as a conduit to the project sponsor with queries on project scope and team remit and authority.

- Resolving conflicts within the team and with their home departments should those departments make undue calls on their representative's time for non-project issues.
- Publishing the completed ITT/SOUR for internal heads of department review and sign-off.
- Agreeing system selection criteria with the selection team and then agreeing these with the project sponsor.
- Identifying, agreeing and approaching potential suppliers with the ITT/SOUR.
- Issuing the ITT/SOUR to potential suppliers and being the conduit with these suppliers for any queries or clarification required. (Note that some potential suppliers will try to circumvent the project manager in an attempt to deal direct with the project sponsor. It should be made clear to them that such an approach will be neither welcome nor tolerated and will be grounds for their exclusion from the process.)
- Leading the selection team in the review and evaluation of responses and the creation of a shortlist.
- Organising demonstrations by selected suppliers and leading the selection team in the evaluation of those demonstrations.
- For each submission; identifying and documenting shortfalls against the ITT/SOUR.
- Providing written recommendations to the project sponsor, along with reasons and estimated costs and timescales.
- Keeping the project sponsor informed of progress and of any issues that may require their involvement.

We will consider the role of the project manager in the implementation phase later.

5.5 The Project Sponsor

The project sponsor is generally the member of senior management who instigated the project in the first place but, if not, will at least be the member of senior management who obtained approval for the expenditure from the Board of Directors. The role necessitates that the holder sits at the most senior level of management within the company. Why is it necessary to have a member of the senior management team as a sponsor? Because the spend on the new system will, depending on the capabilities of the system that you are buying, typically be between one and three per cent of the company's turnover—surely that is worthy of senior management attention?

As with the project manager, the project sponsor must be seen to be treating all departments even-handedly. This gives the project sponsor an immediate problem as she or he is almost certainly the head of a functional area that is part of the implementation. As with the project manager, if members of the team believe any area to be having an unfair or undue influence on the project, they will become demotivated and no longer see the system as a company system but as a departmental system to which they will have to contribute to but to which they will have second-rate access. At that stage you are on a slippery slope to failure.

There is no easy way for the project sponsor to gain the trust of the team that is essential to the success of the project but openness and honesty are good starting points. If there are disagreements that the project sponsor is called upon to adjudicate on, he or she must make visible efforts to listen to all sides, especially if the decision is going to go in their department's favour. Decisions should not be handed down as if they were tablets of stone: the project sponsor should take time to explain the reasons behind them so that the team does not start to fragment.

Before considering the role of the project sponsor in detail, there are two vital functions that the other books don't mention. We will begin this section with one and we will end with one. Firstly, a critical role of the project sponsor is to remove from the project any team member who is not adequately contributing. Reasons why team members don't always pull their weight are generally:

- that they have not sufficiently divorced themselves from their regular function and responsibilities. This is more likely to happen on smaller implementations where team members are not seconded full time, but it happens too on larger projects where team members consider themselves to be indispensable in their primary roles or when departmental emergencies occur. When we look later at the implementation phase, we will consider the concept of 'upward delegation' but, for now, let's just agree that few people can ride two horses at the same time.

- that they feel that they are the one who should have been selected as project manager and are now petulantly doing all they can to make that person's job impossible in the belief that they can then be reconsidered. These people will absent themselves from meetings at short or no notice, deliberately miss deadlines and try constantly to undermine the project manager and the team's confidence in the incumbent. They can be relied upon to be disruptive and to continually make negative statements whilst they sulk.

- that they are just not team players. They will genuinely not be able to see the big picture and will not understand the need for compromise. Frequently it is a case of 'my way or no way'. As with the previous category, they will poison the team spirit that others are trying to build.

- lastly that they lack the knowledge, maturity or intellect necessary to carry out the tasks allocated to them. We mentioned earlier the need to have our best people on the team but, if we have made a mistake, we need to swop people out before they get out of their depth and the project suffers.

Additional responsibilities of the project sponsor include the following.

- Having built the team, it is the responsibility of the project sponsor to define their remit. Does the implementation of a new MRPII/ERP system include the acquisition of hand-held input devices for the sales team, or a new warehousing system, or even a new warehouse? All manner of people will try to slip in pet projects as part of the new system implementation, including projects that have previously been rejected. The project sponsor is responsible for excluding these from the project scope and for ensuring that they stay excluded: a major cause of projects running late, going over budget and missing deadlines is what military types call 'mission creep'. That does not mean that the scope of the project cannot change: only that there should be a formal change control system in place. We will consider this later.

- The project sponsor, being in a senior management role, will know things about the future direction of the company that the team will not. Strategic decisions, such as acquisitions and divestments for example, may be under discussion and it may be premature to make these known in detail to the selection team so it is the sponsor's responsibility to ensure that the chosen system has the ability to cope with these changes.

- It is the job of the project sponsor to protect the team from undue interference. As mentioned before, there may be calls on their time that conflict with project responsibilities. These might be, for example, other projects that are happening simultaneously (something to be avoided) or departmental emergencies. The project manager should deal with these matters on a routine basis but should be able to escalate to the project sponsor any problems that she or he does not have authority to resolve.

- The project sponsor should be the final arbiter on decisions that cannot be agreed by the team. If the team works as a team these should be few but some decisions will cross departmental boundaries and will have to be taken at senior management level.

- The project sponsor, having ultimate responsibility for the success or failure of the project, must satisfy her or himself that the project will meet the company's goals. These goals may shift during the life of the project and it is the sponsor's responsibility to re-target the project should unexpected change occur.

- During the life of the project, the team will experience highs and lows. It is the sponsor's responsibility to pull them back if they get too excited and to gee them up if morale drops. This will necessitate, with the help of the project manager, keeping a finger on the pulse of the team. The project sponsor's role is not reactionary: on the contrary, the project sponsor needs to be proactive and this will necessitate close co-operation with the project manager so that the line between involvement and interference is not crossed.

- Again, because the sponsor assumes ultimate responsibility for the project, he or she must maintain contact with the project via the project manager. Brief daily meetings (15 minutes maximum) backed up by more-formal, minuted weekly meetings are suggested.

- The project team will be delegated responsibility to recommend a solution that is the best achievable fit against the ITT/SOUR that circumstances (i.e. budget and time) permit. The final decision on implementing that decision will rest with the project sponsor and the Board of Directors. Having given permission for the project to move to the implementation phase, delegated responsibility passes back to the project manager and team to deliver the project. However (and this is a very big however), having delivered the project, it is the sponsor's responsibility to ensure that the delivered solution is taken up by the company as a whole. Packaged software is a compromise and, even though they signed off the ITT/SOUR, some departments will drag their feet when it comes to moving onto the new system and some may campaign actively against it. The project team can help to 'sell' the new system internally within the company but, in the face of resistance, it is the responsibility of the project sponsor to ensure, via the Board of Directors if necessary, that the new system is embraced by all departments.

- And now, the promised sting in the tail. In medium and large scale projects, the team members will have been seconded full-time. Of necessity, they will have had to have been replaced in their home departments, either by other departmental colleagues picking up the slack or by temporary replacements. When the project ends, what will the team members be going back to? Will their jobs still exist? Will they be happy to step back out of the limelight? Intelligent team members will want an answer to this question before they sign up. The good news is that, by this stage, you will have a multi-talented team that knows more about the functioning of the company than could ever have been expected. They will be moving forward with a record of success and a belief that they can move mountains. Perhaps you should let them.

5.6 A Project Room

Those of you who have been through implementations know just how important a project room is, so feel free to go for a tea-break now (or skip to the next section). For those of you who have not implemented a sizable system before (word processing and spreadsheets do not count as sizable systems), there are many very good reasons why a project room is not just advantageous but downright essential:

The team needs somewhere to go to think. Working at their desks exposes them to all manner of interruptions and distractions. Especially in a small implementation, where people are only seconded part-time, they need to be focused on the project when working on the project. At their desks, by their phones, they will be tempted, if not forced, to put their regular jobs first and project work will either not get done or, even worse, will be skimped.

The team needs space: they need wall space to post their flow-charts and their to-do lists. They need tables to spread out documents such as ITT/SOURS and responses. They need space to meet with each other and with prospective bidders. They need space to have demonstrations from those bidders and they need space to carry out training; of themselves and of the end-users. If you haven't got a spare conference room that you can hand over for the purpose, the hire of a Portakabin is cheaper than the cost of project failure.

Last but not least: a team room helps engender a team spirit. Having their own space will make them feel like a team and feeling like a team will help them act and think like a team.

But beware: the first time that you evict them from their project room for a 'more important' meeting, you are telling them that they, and their work, are of secondary importance. To what? To a management meeting? To a job interview? To a customer meeting? Think hard before you tell people that their work is secondary.

5.7 Project Justification

Right: you have a team together, you have a project manager in place and you have a project sponsor. You are now ready to spend a lot of money. Let's just pause for a moment though. Whether you are a small company spending £25,000 or a large company spending £10 million, you owe it to yourself and to the company to justify that expenditure.

For some companies, the justification is easy. They have been running an old system that is no longer supportable and the risk to the company of a system failure can no longer be accepted. Or they might be part of a management buy-out and have previously used a corporate system that will no longer be available to them. It might be that the old system has hit a limit, in terms of user count or database size, and can no longer grow with the business. These companies have no choice.

But, for others, remaining with the old system is potentially an option, so the expenditure needs a business justification. You wouldn't invest in new plant without satisfying yourself that, by doing so, you would either make money or save money and the same should be true of an IT investment. What measurable benefit will you get from a new system? It is important to establish criteria not only to justify the expenditure but to have something to measure against when the system goes live. When that day arrives, we will want to know whether the system is achieving what we aimed for. If it is not, then we have to review the situation and decide what we need to do to gain the benefit that we targeted. A new system is not a success just because it is up and running: it needs to pay for itself and the only way to know if it is paying for itself is to measure results.

A frequent justification for a new system is 'improved management information' but this is not measurable and, anyway, unless such information finds its way to the bottom line as improved profits, it is of no value. It might make our lives easier and our jobs more fun (and there is certainly nothing wrong with that), but it is not a justification and is certainly not measurable.

So, improved stock control is not a valid target but reducing stock levels by 20% is. Improving cash flow is not a valid target but reducing debtor days by 10% is. Having a better picture of what is on the shopfloor is not a valid target but reducing manufacturing lead times by 10% is. (Note, by the way, that I said manufacturing lead times and not delivery lead times. Unless you have infinite capacity, the only way to get delivery lead times down and keep them down is to sell less! The reason is that, when you have finite capacity, there is a finite limit to how much the factory can produce. If you sell more than the factory can produce, your delivery lead times will go out. It's as simple as that; so don't put reduced delivery lead times on your justification.)

Having listed your targets, do your sums. Will the increased profit that hitting those targets will achieve be enough to pay for the investment required? If yes; go ahead. If not; stop. Blind faith is not enough.

5.8 The ITT/SOUR

A written statement of what the new system is required to deliver is essential to achievement of a successful project but is one of the hardest things to do. At the one extreme, it should not be a list of generalities such as "improved management information" or "increased service levels" but, on the other hand, it should not be so detailed that prospective bidders give up on trying to read it!

The length of the document that you should send to prospective bidders is very much dependent upon the size of the contract that you are offering. If you are looking for a multi-million pounds sterling JBOPS system, you can expect the bidders to do a lot of work to win your business but, if you are a small company with twenty thousand pounds to spend, you cannot expect more than one or two days of the bidder's time. Give such a bidder a document that takes several days or weeks to respond to and their cost of sale will be higher than their anticipated profit, meaning that only the companies most desperate for work will respond. Ask yourself why they are so desperate for work that they will take a contract that will lose them money. If you really need a detailed document for assessment purposes (and I mean *really* need), then consider a cut down version for external purposes.

Formal ITT/SOUR documents have unfortunately fallen out of favour in recent years. The reason is that so many of them were bad and unfit for purpose. Problems included:

- An inappropriate level of detail; being too detailed or too sketchy.
- A failure to reflect the business's true wants and needs because they were written by people (generally, but not always, external consultants) who did not really understand what was wanted. Many documents were, in fact, taken from a 'stock' of previously-used ITT/SOURs, cut and pasted into a notionally bespoke document. The results were simultaneously poor and expensive.
- A failure to look into the future. No one can predict the future with any certainty but, when preparing an ITT/ SOUR, we should not just specify what we want and need today but we must make some sort of allowance for where the business is likely to be going in the medium term. Are there expectations that you will be opening foreign subsidiaries that might need foreign language versions of the software? Are there expectations that you will be setting up a maintenance

division to offer after sales service? It is impossible to totally future-proof a system but we owe it to ourselves to try.

The other big problem with ITT/SOURs is that they have traditionally been page upon page of tick boxes. Let me demonstrate the weakness of this. Some years ago, I worked with a very good MRPII system that had what was for some companies a serious flaw. Although it was a multi-currency system, all sales price lists were held in one base currency and translated into other currencies at the time of transaction at an exchange rate that could be re-set periodically. For example, my base price for an item might be £1,000 and my exchange rate to USD 1.50 so my invoice would be for $1,500. However, exchange rates tend not to be static and, on my next sale, the rate of exchange may have moved to, say, 1.60 giving a sales price of $1,600 and not $1,500. Some companies are happy with this but most are not. They issue price lists in different currencies and their customers expect to be invoiced the price that is on the price list.

The problem that I then had, in responding to ITT/SOURs, was that many of these had a question along the lines of, "Is your system multi-currency?", with a tick-box that only allowed a yes or no answer. One such question in an ITT/SOUR does not pose an insurmountable problem but hundreds do. So a good ITT/SOUR needs to come at the problem from a totally different angle. In the above example, I should not have been asked a question that asked for a Y/N answer: it would have been better for the customer to have asked, "How does your system handle multi-currency transactions?".

Now, the down-side to this, of course, is that such answers, being more-detailed, take more time for the bidder to write and more time for the customer to read. There must then be fewer questions on the ITT/SOUR. In actuality, this is not really a problem. Old-fashioned documents were full of questions such as "How many characters are there in the customer name field?" and "Is there a field for the buyer's initials on the stock file?" so let's consider what a useful (to both customer and bidder) ITT/SOUR should look like.

The first section should describe the business and what it does. It should proffer the following information:

- Name and address of the Company.
- Locations of off-site facilities such as out-rigger factories, warehouses and subsidiaries that will be using the system. If any of these are abroad and require screens or reports in different languages, this should be stated.
- The company's line of business; eg "Manufacture of upholstered furniture for home market and export", "Design and manufacture of electronics for the aircraft industry", "Manufacture and distribution through regional warehouses of consumer electrical products".
- Are you a make-to-stock, make-to-order, assemble-to-order or design-to-order company? Or a hybrid of two or three of these?
- The size of the company; both an indication of turn-over and of number of staff.
- Some basic statistics: how many products do you have, how many orders do you typically process in a week etc.
- What is important to the business or, to ask the question a different way, why do your customers come to you and not your competitors? Are your prices lower? Are your delivery

lead-times shorter? Is your quality and reliability better? (If you answered 'yes' to the above three questions, by the way, you are probably about to go out of business as your costs must be higher than the competition that you are under-cutting.)

- If there is a requirement to link to other systems, and these are needs and not nice-to-haves, then give brief details of these other systems.

- Lastly, give contact details for the project manager (and explicitly not for the project sponsor).

One primary reason for this section is that, although bidders can never know your business, it will help you and them if they can at least begin to understand it. This section should fit into one page. The second page should show the following:

- An indication of budget. If you state that your budget is £10 million, small suppliers will know not to waste their time and, by doing so, not waste yours. If you state that your budget is £10,000 then large outfits will know not to waste their time and, by doing so, not waste yours.

- Projected timescales. Perhaps the new system has to be in and ready for the beginning of the new financial year, for example.

- Anything that would be a genuine show-stopper. For example, your French subsidiary needs screens in French, or you are part of a group of companies and you must stick to corporate standards on databases etc. Anything that is listed as being non-negotiable must be justified to the project sponsor **and** to the team. Some people hold that the length of the part number is sacrosanct or that that the new system should be compatible with the old Chart of Accounts structure but I would argue not. Ask yourself; if you found a system that was a perfect fit in every other area, would you not renumber your parts; would you not restructure your Chart of Accounts? Of course you would. If your argument is that it is too much work or too difficult; justify that view to the rest of the team but remember that you might be setting a precedent.

Following these introductory chapters, each functional area should specify what they need from the new system. As we said before, this should not be a list of database fields, nor a list of required reports (most systems nowadays provide means for writing your own reports anyway: in fact some popular and expensive systems are delivered with no standard reports at all). This part of the ITT/SOUR should describe the way that each department works and the business processes that the system must support. It should then ask the prospective bidders how their system can contribute to those objectives. The document must be specific about what needs to be done but should not specify how it is to be done.

One very common mistake, as we said before, is to document the current system and use that as a basis of our requirements. If we bought cars that way, we would still be driving Model 'T' Fords. If we get into too much detail, we will find ourselves too much constrained by our previous experiences. If we tell prospective bidders what we are trying to achieve, as opposed to what we are trying to do, then they, having implemented systems at many other companies and knowing their software well, may be able to suggest alternative and better ways of doing things. We should not close the door to free consultancy, knowing that the choice of whether or not we accept subsequent recommendations is ours and ours alone.

We also need to ensure that the document lists all of our business processes and not just the ones that are causing problems today. We can, in writing the document, too easily forget the things that are working fine and assume that the new system will do all that the old system did. Even if your new system is coming from the same supplier as your old one, this is almost certainly not the case. The reason is that systems go through three stages in their lifetime:

1. Immaturity

Writing a new system takes a lot of time and money (it is difficult to give an average for systems that cost between ten thousand pounds and ten million pounds but a medium size system has probably had in the region of 300 man-years invested in it). To fund that investment, the system must be brought to market as soon as it is sellable and that means that, although mainstream functionality can be expected, there will be notable gaps in functionality in areas that are not core. For example, you can expect to be able to raise and transact purchase orders but there might not initially be facilities for handling requisitions or consignment stocks.

2. Maturity

As this stage, the system will satisfy most user companies. Major gaps will have been plugged but some niche functionality will still be missing in non-core areas; perhaps such as capacity scheduling, engineering change control or maintenance management.

3. Obsolescence

In this stage, the system has most of the functionality that will ever be built into it and reasonable work-arounds will be available to cover any weaknesses. However, it will now be starting to look tired when compared to newer systems. Remember just a few years ago when character-based (or green screen) systems were the norm. Then people got used to PC-type interfaces and overnight green screen looked old-fashioned. Sales were lost to newer (immature) systems with less functionality and, although authors of mature systems tried to make them look more modern, and introduced more modern interfaces, largely they were forced to develop their own new (and initially immature) systems on order to be competitive and to give the market what it wanted. So the cycle re-starts.

The rule is that nothing is there until you have checked that it is there. No functionality is there unless you have confirmed it. Nothing can be assumed or taken for granted. The name on the package might be the same but the content almost certainly differs.

The question then is what level of detail the ITT/SOUR should get into. We have already alluded to this by saying that the amount of time that we can expect from bidders is directly related to the size of the contract offered. I would have no hesitation in handing a 200 page document to a bidder for a £10 million system but, for a £10,000 system I would not expect anyone to read and respond to a document of more than ten or twenty pages. Likewise I would expect a detailed response for a large system but not for a small. Given the range of systems on the market, it is impossible to give an indication of what you can expect for a specific budget but, as a very crude rule of thumb, I would say around a day for every £50,000 to cover an ITT/SOUR response and subsequent demonstration for a medium size system, although this will not be accurate as we move towards either end of the spectrum. Depending on the amount of work that they already have on their books, some software companies may be more or less generous.

5.9 ITT/SOUR Issue

When issuing ITT/SOURs to prospective bidders, the temptation is to take a scatter gun approach and believe that, the more suppliers we contact, the better chance of getting a good result. However, the workload that you will be generating for yourself in doing that will be utterly disproportion to the results achieved. You might feel good about sending out fifty 200-page ITT/SOURs but, believe me, you won't feel good when fifty documents come back for evaluation.

Experience says that you are unlikely to be able to cope properly with more than about four to six; probably half that in the case of a big system like one of the JBOPS. The reason is not just the amount of time required to adequately read and analyse the responses but the fact, and it is a fact, that if you are dealing with a large number of responses, you will not be able to compare them properly and will get utterly confused. Believe me: six is enough.

But which software suppliers to select? We have already discussed the danger of being led by consultants but, with caution, they are a place to start. Just make sure that you ask them for more than one. There are, of course, the regular software shows where you will have the advantage of bouncing your budget off suppliers and seeing how they react: there is no point in sending an ITT/SOUR to a JBOPS supplier if your budget is £50,000 for example. If going to such a show, do not get carried away and sign up for a system there and then, regardless of how good it looks. Only a proper evaluation and comparison will do.

As we said earlier; an under-used source of suggestions are your business partners: your customers and suppliers. Some of them must be of similar size and have similar requirements to you. You will also have a number of contacts through professional bodies if only you think to approach them. People will be remarkably willing to help.

When you send out your ITT/SOURs, be aware that prospective bidders are likely to have queries and items that need clarification. Allow time in the process for this to happen. It is not a bad thing, as it shows that the bidders are reading the documents properly. Also, when one supplier queries something, wonder why the others didn't. Perhaps it indicates that they have a better understanding of your needs but perhaps it indicates that they haven't read the document properly. Ensure that the project manager is always the conduit for these conversations so that the process is properly controlled and monitored.

One last thought on the ITT/SOUR: all bidders will be trying to show their own system in the best possible light. Good outfits will not tell lies in their responses but even the best will interpret questions advantageously. This is one reason why we said that questions that ask for Y/N answers should be avoided wherever possible. However, make it clear to the bidders that any response to the ITT/SOUR will be written into the contract so that they are not tempted to push their luck too far.

5.10 Evaluation of Responses

We have used the word 'measurable' frequently so it will be no surprise that we want to measure the responses. It is the only way to compare them, against each other and against our needs. There are two ways of scoring responses and we will look at both of them.

In the first method, responses to individual questions are rated on a scale of zero to 10, with zero meaning that the software cannot support the requirement and 10 saying that it is a perfect fit. In the middle is a grey area: maybe the system supports it but not very well or maybe is can support it with modifications. Responses that fall into these categories get a score between 1 and 9 depending on the assessed fit or amount of modification required. Having scored all requirements, the scores are totalled and the systems with the highest totals are put on the short list.

This appears logical but there are two problems. First; any score between 1 and 9 is largely subjective. Is something that doesn't fit very well a 3 or a 7? How can we assess the size, and therefore cost of any modification? Some people say that, with a team of six or so doing separate assessments, the fluctuations will even out. But this means that we are asking production people to assess fit in financial areas, finance people in sales areas and sales people in purchasing areas. Yes; each team member could take each response back to his or her home department for assessment, and the bidders could be asked to give an indication of modification cost but is the first likely to be viable and the second likely to be accurate? Probably not. The result will be that systems that are a great fit in almost areas, but totally lacking in others, will win out over systems that are average throughout. This may seem to be right but what if the winning systems, in a small number of areas, lack functionality that cannot be satisfied by modifications and these areas are mission critical? We could be putting on the short list systems that cannot meet our essential requirements. That and its inherent subjectivity make this a less than ideal way to go.

The alternative is to go for a traffic light system, where green says OK, red says it can't be done and amber is 'grey'! Having scored each requirement thus, we assess the red areas to confirm that these are definitely things that we cannot do without. If we can't do without them and a bidder can't supply them, that bid is off the list regardless of how good it is in other areas. If we get to the end of the six responses and all bids have failed, we have to ask ourselves if we are being realistic. Are we asking for too much? Do we have champagne tastes and beer budgets? If something cannot be done by any system and it is a mandatory business requirement, then the only option is to handle it offline. We could send out another six ITT/SOURs to new bidders but we would likely be wasting our time.

At some stage, however, we will have a short list of ideally, for small and medium systems, three or four potential suppliers who will be asked to demonstrate their offerings. In the case of larger (JBOPS) systems, we are unlikely to be able to assess properly more than two so the rules have to change. With those heavyweights, invite in only the two most likely. This is not ideal but is more practical. Assessing JBOPS systems is extremely difficult because of their size. Most of these large systems need weeks and months of configuration to fit your company's needs (they are effectively a set of building blocks) and the bidders simply won't be able to do that for a demonstration. The result is that, in many areas, you will be asked to take things on trust ("The system is being used by Megacorp, Inc so, believe me, it will work for you."). Don't.

Whether you are buying a small, medium or large system, as much as possible should be demonstrated to you within the time available (note the previous comments about how much time you can expect bidders to make available to you). During all meetings and demonstrations, all claims and statements should be noted and a written communication sent to the bidders along the lines of, "This is what we understood you to say. Please confirm our understanding in writing so that your response can be incorporated into the contract." If their responses are vague and imprecise, walk away: they are vague and imprecise for a reason. They are being economical with the truth again.

But we are jumping ahead of ourselves again.

We now have a short list of two to four possible suppliers. The project manager should now contact those companies to arrange demonstrations. If you are having more than one demonstration, leave time between them so that each offering can be fully assessed before turning your attention to the next. The reason is that if you see several demonstrations, they will merge into a blur. Trust me: I have been complimented by customers on demonstrations that I never gave! Don't leave too big a gap, though, in case you get to the end of number three and can't remember number one. A few days should suffice.

The demonstration can take place anywhere where there is enough room and where interruptions and distractions can be guaranteed not to happen but, if they take place in the project room, take care to ensure that commercially sensitive information is not displayed on the wall. It should be made clear to people that it is not acceptable for them to drift in and out of demonstrations and it is not acceptable for them to have their mobile phones switched on either. If you think that taking a phone call from the President of the United States in the middle of a meeting will impress people, just think how much more impressive it would be to refuse to take such a call.

When it comes to the demonstration itself, it is a great help to have some of your own data loaded to the demo system as some team members will not be able to conceptualise and will need to see their own products being bought, made and sold. However; be realistic about how much the bidders can load. Don't expect to see all of your company data loaded; a representative selection will suffice—if you can make three products, you can make three hundred, if you can sell to one home customer and one export customer, you can sell to one hundred.

When organising the demonstration, the bidders should have been told what you need and expect to see. That check list should be in front of you throughout the demonstration. The bidders will be trying to demonstrate their software's strengths and hide its weaknesses so will want to keep to their own pre-prepared agenda or script. That's fine as long as, when you get to the end of the demo, all of your points have been covered. If they haven't, and you have run out of time, the project manager should tell the bidder what has not been demonstrated. At that stage the bidder should be given two choices: to say in writing that the system does what you want, the way you want to do it, without chargeable modification, or to allow you to assume that it cannot. However nice they are, however good a relationship you think you have with them, you should not be asked to take anything on trust: after all, they will be asking you to sign a written contract, will they not? I am sure that they do not expect you to think that a verbal promise that the system will be paid for is the basis of a sound business relationship. In a good business relationship, a contract works both ways.

One last word of caution. Some demonstrations can be 'smoke and mirrors' so, even if you think you have seen something, if it is critical, write down what you think you saw and have the bidder confirm it in writing. As we said before; although external consultants should not be in charge of the selection process, if they are good enough and experienced enough, they should be able to read between the lines of a demonstration and ask for clarification and for confirmation when necessary.

Remember that the purpose of the demonstration is not to confirm that you are dealing with nice guys, or to admire their presentation skills, or to be impressed by their customer list or their corporate facilities. It is to demonstrate that their software does what you need it to do. Nothing else is relevant and you can be sure that more 'fluff' they show you, the less functionality they have to back up their claims.

5.11 Selection and contract placement

At the end of the demonstration phase, the project manager and selection team should retire to their project room and compare notes. Whilst it is undeniably important that the quality of a software vendor's implementation team is key to a successful implementation, the first step has to be to assess the software itself. The only way to assess the systems that have been demonstrated to you is to go through the ITT/SOUR line by line and assess each item as green, grey or red. Don't at this stage spend too much time on the greys, as the first pass is really to find the reds: i.e. the areas that each package cannot support.

For an item to be marked green, you must be certain that you either witnessed it clearly demonstrated (remember the previous comments about smoke and mirrors) or you have a statement in writing from the system supplier guaranteeing that the system does what you want, how you want, without chargeable modification. Items which the software suppliers advised would require chargeable modification, or which were not demonstrated but are awaiting written confirmation should be flagged amber, as should items that appeared workable but cumbersome. Those items that the software cannot address are clearly red. It is advantageous for the team to go through this assessment together as frequently different people pick up on different things during a long demonstration and some things will, in any case, straddle departmental boundaries.

Each team member should lead the assessment of his or her prime area and advise the team of their assessment on each point, along with reasons why. It is the job of the team, and the project manager, to challenge any assessment that they disagree with; again with reasons why. At the end of the process it is possible, but very unlikely, that one competing system will have no reds but, as I have never seen this happen in over twenty years, I am for the moment going to ignore the possibility. In fact, if you have no reds at all, I would worry about your selection criteria and process.

More likely, if you were reviewing four to six systems, some at least will have fewer reds than others and some more, so you should get your shortlist down to a couple or so. If you are reviewing two JBOPS systems, perhaps one will score slightly better than the other. Having scored reds against criteria that you regarded as being essential, you will be tempted to go around again, with another selection of potential suppliers. Experience says that you will be wasting your time because, if there was an ideal system out there, there would only be one system out there!

So the next thing to do is to go through the reds, as a team, and challenge whether each of those criteria really is non-negotiable. Our friend Confucius also said, "The best is the enemy of the good". That means that if you continue searching for a perfect system, you will never implement a good one. Hopefully the second pass will have turned some reds to amber so it is now time to consider what to do about the ones that remain.

Option 1 is to request quotations for modifications from the various suppliers. As we said before, if you are potentially spending a lot of money with a supplier, you can expect that supplier to spend a reasonable amount of time in estimating the time, and thence the cost, of any modifications required. Be aware, though, that quoting accurately for modifications takes more time and money that you imagine, so suppliers are likely to come back with ball park figures rather than firm quotes if the list is too long. Even rough estimates, though, will give you a feel for whether the likely cost of the modifications is something that you can live with. Remember, though, that the suppliers want your business and may be tempted to quote low in the knowledge that once you have bought the system there will be not much that you can do when, having looked in detail at your requirements, they come up with a substantially higher figure. See also the earlier comments about the true cost of bespoke modifications.

Option 2 is to ask the suppliers how other companies that they have worked with handle these problems. They may have acceptable work–arounds in place.

The last option is to look at handling those requirements off-line, either through manual systems such as spreadsheets or via specialist sub-systems; for example in the case of capacity scheduling or engineering change control.

All of this will take time and money (yours and the suppliers') so don't be offended or surprised if some suppliers 'qualify out': that is to say that they take a business decision not to proceed with their bid because they can see the cost of getting your business to be too high.

When you have finished your analysis and obtained written confirmation of all of the promises that were made to you but not demonstrated, you are in a position to narrow-down your short list. Now, having been objective all the way through the process, I have to ask you to make subjective decisions on perhaps the most important thing: the ability and integrity of the people that you may be signing a contract with. This is all the more difficult because, the larger the company that you are dealing with, the less likely that the people that you have met during the selection phase will be around for the implementation. That is because the larger companies will have dedicated sales and pre-sales people and the people who demonstrated the system to you are likely to be full time analysts and demonstrators. Without doubt, if these companies employ turkeys, you won't see them during the demonstration phase.

How do you gauge the ability of people that you haven't met? Well; you can ask to see the CVs of the people likely to be working on your project but, depending on the amount of work that your supplier has on the books, they may not be able to guarantee the availability of particular people, especially before there is a detailed project plan and timescale in existence. Quite simply; other companies may sign up before you and it is unrealistic to expect suppliers to 'reserve' staff in the hope that your contract firms up. All you can do is to get a feel for the type of staff that the company employs but do feel free to ask to meet a selection of their people even if telephone conversations are the best that can be managed.

You should also have the chance of reference site visits or at least telephone calls. Obviously, prospective suppliers will not take you to their problem sites where people can be expected to say bad things about them but you can improve your chances of having a productive meeting by planning ahead. Consider what it is that you want to hear, remembering that they will be pre-disposed to saying nice things. As with the ITT/SOUR, asking questions that invite a yes or no answer will not be the most productive. For example, I know that businesses are comprised of human beings and human beings make mistakes. The companies that I am loyal to are not companies that have never made mistakes: they are the ones which rectify mistakes in a professional manner.

So don't ask the reference sites if they are happy with the software and happy with the supplier—you know what the answer will be. Instead, ask them what problems and difficulties they had and how they were overcome. Ask them what their implementation timescales were and how many training and consultancy days they had. Ask them what measured results they have achieved. By doing that, you will get a lot nearer the truth.

Having gathered up all the facts and taken as many references as you can get, the team must decide which of the systems that they have reviewed offers the best chance of success. It is nice when this is a unanimous decision but it rarely is and this is where the project manager and project sponsor have an important role to play in reminding the team that they are looking for the best system for the company as a whole and not just for individual departments. As we said before, this requires intelligence and maturity on the part of the team members, even though you will have stressed 'the rules of the game' at the very beginning of the project.

Some companies try to get around the problem by leaving the decision in the hands of the project manager or project sponsor but this is not a good idea. If the team are not part of the decision, they won't own it and the last thing that you can afford when you move into the implementation phase is a team who are implementing a system that they do not regard as 'theirs'.

If you have a big enough team, a points based system can be the answer but be aware that, in a small team, some immature members may try to weight things in their favour by scoring their choice unrealistically high and the others unfairly low. The scoring should be carried out by the team together so that each score can be challenged. Because you will be considering the estimated cost of bespoke modifications also, this will have to be factored into the decision. Generally the best way to handle this is to score the systems on the basis of no modifications, then again with modifications and to ask if the cost of the modifications is justifiable. Don't rush this decision: it is better to take days or even weeks on it than to make a mistake.

When the team has made a decision and obtained accurate costings, the project manager should gather all of the information together and provide a written report, including recommendations, to the project sponsor. This report should include detail on what the new system is *not* able to cover and how the team thinks that these shortcomings can be managed. It should be followed up by a formal meeting between the team and the project sponsor when the sponsor can question and challenge the team about their choice. The purpose of this meeting is to give the project sponsor the knowledge and confidence to take these recommendations to the highest level of management for sign off.

Some companies feel it sufficient for the project sponsor to sign off the proposal but it is not. The choice will have been a compromise and the decision may not have been unanimous. Doubtless, if the system chosen was not the choice of their departmental representative on the selection team, heads of department will know it. But the management team, and the selection team, must adhere to the rules of cabinet responsibility—when the decision is announced to the rest of the company, they must all support it visibly and without reservation. If just one head of department goes back to their team and says, "It's not the system that I would have chosen . . .", then the project is on a slippery slope to failure.

If any head of department feels unable to accept the new system, they need to say so now before the contract is signed. If there are dissenters on the board, the CEO must listen to the arguments and then decide whether the election team has to go around the loop again. Once the decision is taken, though, it must be final and no equivocations or reservations must ever find their way out of that room. If people don't believe that their boss believes in the new system, the chances are that neither will they, and implementing a system that people don't believe in, on a difficulty scale of one to ten, is an eleven.

You are almost ready to sign the contract with you chosen system supplier and you should advise them of your intent. With that knowledge, they should now be prepared to invest some of their time in firming-up the estimates that they gave you for any bespoke modifications. These need to be written into the contract, along with the written assurances that you requested about functionality that was promised but which, for whatever reason, could not be demonstrated. If your supplier will not agree to this; walk away.

A formal 'thank you' to the selection team is now required. It does not have to cost anything (in fact, it is better if it doesn't) but a five-minute meeting in the sponsor's office to acknowledge their efforts will go a long way in the implementation phase and may also go some way towards smoothing the ruffled feathers of team members whose first choice system wasn't the one selected.

6. Implementation

6.1 Big bang or phased?

The first question that you have to ask yourself is how you are going to implement the software. Particularly on large implementations, some people prefer a phased approach: perhaps starting with the financial modules then moving through the distribution modules and finishing with manufacturing. Arguments for this are:

- If anything goes wrong, the risk to the company is minimised as the functional areas not in that phase are unaffected.
- At any one time, there are fewer balls in the air and so attention can be more focused.
- If you start with the easy and straight-forward areas first, confidence rises and makes subsequent work easier.
- The answer to the question of how to eat an elephant is, "One piece at a time".

But, countering that, there are problems with a phased approach:

- The implementation takes several times longer (some would say that the pain goes on for longer).
- Costs are higher.

Let's look at those points in detail to decide their possible effect on your implementation.

The implementation takes longer.

One obvious disadvantage of a phased approach is that the benefits of having a company-wide integrated system are delayed. A phased implementation means about a trebling of implementation time; sometimes more. That means that the increased efficiency that justified the expenditure on the software will not arrive for months or years later than could have been the case. Things will happen in those intervening months or years: members of the implementation team will move on, other projects will start up and will compete for money and resources, new managers will come in with different ideas and will want changes.

More damagingly, people will get tired and it will get harder and harder to keep the enthusiasm and momentum going. The implementation will be in real danger of just fizzling out before it is completed, and you will be left with half a system and a forest of spreadsheets and manual systems. Frequently there will be no formal decision to halt the implementation and it may even become a comfortable institution, with some team members happy to continue having regular meetings in a comfortable room with coffee and biscuits even though nothing results.

Costs are higher.

Increased costs will be experienced in several areas. You are going to have consultants around for much longer. True; there will be fewer of them on site at any one time but, if they are there a long time, having them can become a habit that is hard to break. There will always be opportunities to find them more to do and, believe me, they will be actively looking for more work themselves.

Another thing to consider is the cost of having key people tied up on the project for longer than is necessary. Even if it is only a case of missed opportunities to use them elsewhere, there is a cost.

Re-work is another consideration. The longer the project goes on, the more chance that new managers will come into the company with different ideas on what is required. I once saw an expediting sub-system go through three changes of manager during its gestation: needless to say, it never went live.

Leaving the big one until last; the costs incurred in running two systems is obviously greater than running one. You may have continuing support charges on your old system and hardware. You will definitely have greater data entry costs, as many transactions cross departmental boundaries. For example, if the first phase of the implementation is the financial area, you are going to be raising and receipting purchase orders in your old system and processing supplier invoices in your new. All manner of interim manual procedures will have to be put in place to keep both system synchronised. These procedure will require extra work and, inevitably, extra staff.

One last thought on phased implementations. We said earlier that, in a phased implementation, it makes sense for the financial ledgers to go in first. Even if you are careful to ensure that your finance department does not have a disproportionate influence in the way the system is set up (and it is very difficult for the lead department not to have a disproportionate influence, regardless of which department it is), there is a very real danger that the rest of the company will see it as being primarily a finance system. Indeed, in one implementation of an MRPII system that I did, the head of the finance department, at the project kick off meeting, told the audience of middle managers from across the company that the company was putting in "a new accounting system" but then assured them that "they would be able to get useful information out of it too". I have never seen so many people switch off so quickly and so visibly.

6.2 People

The team in the implementation phase must be the same as in the selection phase. People will be more driven to get the system working successfully if they are simultaneously justifying their choice. There is, though, scope for extra members to be drafted in to work on specific tasks under the supervision of the core implementation team. It will be advantageous to set up teams to look at things like bills of material accuracy, lot sizing etc. Drafting in people helps with subsequent buy-in to the completed system; as the more people who feel that it is 'their' system, the better chance of success.

The roles of the project manager and project sponsor remain essentially the same but they now have increased responsibility to prevent mission creep. With a high profile (and costly) project under way, it will be easy for people to dump problems on the project team's doorstep. Passing the buck is much easier than solving problems, so you will hear phrases such as, "Surely this problem is one of the things that the new system has been bought to solve", and "Surely the MRPII implementation team can look at this as part of the project". I guess that any sentence that begins with a "Surely" is suspect. A good rule is that people should only approach the implementation with solutions and not problems (and spending a million is not a solution—it is a problem).

As mentioned before; other vital roles of the project sponsor are maintaining the morale of the team when things get tough, and ensuring that all heads of department not only support the project but do so visibly and loudly. No one said that this was going to be easy.

6.3 Training

You must be sick of me saying this by now but, with training, as with many other things, you have options. Essentially, you can have your software supplier train your end users or you can go for a train-the-trainer approach, whereby the software supplier trains your implementation team who then become responsible for disseminating that knowledge throughout the company.

Some people prefer that the software supplier carries out end-user training for the following reasons:

- It allows the implementation team to concentrate on developing new procedures and ways of working.

- The system supplier's staff should have an in-depth knowledge of the system and are less likely to be caught out by detailed questions.

My personal preference is for a train-the-trainer approach, for the following reasons:

- Your software supplier will have good knowledge of the way that the system works but your own people should have a better idea of how it is actually going to be used in your company. They can take knowledge from the supplier and translate that into language and terms that your own people will understand better.

- The implementation team need to know more than the end-users. They must understand all of the options available so that, if things change in the future, they can re-tune the system to a changing environment. For example, I have worked with a system that offered half a dozen different ways of booking materials into stock and, whilst the team needs to know and understand all of those, your people in the warehouse will only want to know the one that has been chosen as being best for the way your company works.

- If your team does the end-user training, they will gain enhanced status and the trust and respect of the end-users.

- In the words of Confucius again; "To teach is to learn twice". Believe me; you may think that you know something but, having taught it, you *really* know it.

Remember, though, that the ability to train is a skill that not everyone has. We have all known very intelligent, very knowledgeable people who just do not have what it takes to be good teachers. Some lack the necessary patience, some find it difficult to put concepts and ideas into words, some lack the confidence to stand up in front of their peers and take questions and some just lack social skills and therefore alienate their audience. All of these can be overcome but remember that, if you take the train-the-trainer route, you may have to train your trainers how to train.

Whichever method you decide on, there is a golden rule. That is that training should never, ever take place at users' desks: there are quite simply too many distractions. What will the people being trained do when their phone rings or when someone comes up with an 'urgent' query or request? If you insist that you have to train people at their desks, be aware that experience says that a good rule of thumb is that only around a third of their time will be spent on actually learning, so factor that into the time that you are scheduling. In other words; if the advice you get from your software supplier is that one day is required for a particular element of training, allow three days if the users are getting that training at their desks.

We have covered training very early in this chapter because it is vital that your implementation team get it very early on in the implementation phase so that they can move on to developing new ways of working with the system. Training of end-users, on the other hand, should be left until much later, however keen they are to have it. The team needs to decide which options are to be used and how they are to be used and, if the end-users get trained too early, they will forget much of what they have learned before they get a chance to put it into practice.

6.4 The project plan

Implementing even a small system involves many more tasks than you might imagine. Not only is it essential that all tasks are carried out, but it is frequently essential that they are carried out in the correct order. For example, there is no point scheduling the loading of the software to take place before your server has been delivered and there is no point in scheduling training to take place before vital bespoke modifications are ready. And if your people will be using bespoke elements of software, it is plainly essential that those elements are in place, and have been rigorously tested, before training takes place. It can also be embarrassing when expensive consultants turn up and nobody is ready for them. Lastly, people need to know what is going to happen and when it is going to happen.

For those reasons, a written project plan is essential. In a small implementation, you can get away with a spreadsheet-based plan and this has the added advantage of being easy to distribute. For larger projects, a purpose-designed project management software package can still be very cheap and has the advantage of allowing conflicts in resource usage to be easily identified: have people been scheduled to take part in two training sessions simultaneously or have two training sessions been booked for the one training room on the same day? In surprisingly small projects, these things happen; believe me.

An added advantage of a proper project plan is that it allows timescales to be properly assessed. If a plan requires large numbers of your financial people to be available for training over a financial month end, is that practical and sensible? If it requires particular end-users to attend training sessions on three or four days of a particular week, can this actually be achieved? A detailed project plan is the only way that you can ensure that the right people are available at the right time and the only way that you can measure progress. How else can the project manager and project sponsor be confident that milestones will be achieved on time and within budget?

Remember that your system supplier should be able to help you get a plan together. They will know how long training in their software takes and will most likely have implemented it in companies of similar size and with similar needs to your own. Even a look at someone else's plan from a successful implementation will give you an idea of the level of detail required.

6.5 Change control procedures

This section is placed immediately after project planning for good reason. The project plan states what you are going to do: anything in the plan will get done, whilst anything not in the plan will not get done. The project plan and the ITT/SOUR together define the scope of the system, but we have already acknowledged that all sorts of people will try to expand or change the scope of the project, and for all sorts of reasons. It is unwise to just bolt the door against all requests, as some of them may be valid. During the course of the project, the implementation team itself may come across important things that were missed, whilst some things that were planned to happen may turn out to be unworkable.

Some changes or additions can seem trivial but it is necessary for all of them to be properly assessed in case solving a problem in one area then causes a problem in another. Additionally, little changes mount up. I know that, as a consultant, if I had reacted to every request that began, "Whilst you are here" or "Can you just", then implementation times and costs would soon have gone out of control. So a proper procedure has to be put in place.

However minor the change or addition appears to be (and they will frequently turn out to be bigger than anticipated), each must be justified in writing and sent to the project sponsor for approval. The project sponsor must be aware that every change and addition adds cost and time to the project, and therefore also risk; so the sponsors approval must not just be a rubber stamp. The cost and impact of each must be carefully assessed with the help of the project manager and perhaps the system supplier's consultants.

6.6 Communication

Communication during the project takes many forms. The project sponsor and the project manager should formally meet for a minuted meeting once a week. In addition, the whole team should have a brief stand-up meeting every day to discuss problems and progress. What is a stand-up meeting? It is just the same as an ordinary meeting but with the rule that nobody can sit down. You will be surprised how much shorter meetings become! The rules also say that meetings start on time and any decisions taken before late comers arrive cannot be re-taken without a written request to the project sponsor. The assumption must be that, if something is important, it is worth turning up on time at the meeting for.

Whilst we are about it; let's now also introduce the rule of upward delegation. Whether it is for training or meetings, you are going to have instances when people just do not turn up and the reason given will be that they are too busy, that there is an emergency that they absolutely have to attend to, or that they are ill. In these circumstances, people generally send a deputy but this is a waste of time. What happens when a deputy attends is that, if decisions get made, when the deputy reports back to his or her boss, the boss frequently expects and demands a right of veto on the grounds that they were not consulted. They also expect training to be re-done; especially if they think that their deputy didn't ask enough questions or didn't always understand the answers. The result is a hideous waste of time, as meetings and training sessions have to be re-convened. Now; I accept that emergencies can happen and people can be ill and we have to deal with it, which is where upward delegation comes in.

Here is the scenario: if I am genuinely unable to attend a meeting or training session, my boss should agree that the circumstances that prevent me being there are unavoidable. In those circumstances, my boss will attend in my place. Of course, my boss may not agree with my reasons for not being able to attend, in which case he or she can take whatever measures are necessary to enable me to be there. The result is that the project continues on schedule and does not become a series of U-turns that frustrates the team to the point that they give up.

In addition to communication between the various elements of the team, there is a continuing need for communication with the rest of the company. There is the danger that the team could be seen as a private club which at some stage will hand down new systems and procedures to end-users as if they were tablets of stone. People not directly involved with the implementation need to know what is going on and, if you don't tell them, the rumour mill will. A routine newsletter is a cheap and effective way of keeping people in touch so that they have time to get used to the idea of a new system and are less likely to resist it.

Whatever way you choose to communicate, although the aim will be to be positive about the new system, you must be open and honest about problems that are being encountered. You can't hide them so don't try. Most problems, as we will see in the chapter 'What can go wrong?', are people problems, so don't allow the system to be blamed for delays and problems unfairly because, if you do, you will be weakening confidence in the team's ability to deliver a good system. If delays are caused by people changing their minds or not hitting targets, say so. If you have found gaps in what the system can do, say so but also say what you are doing about it. If you allow communication by rumour, don't be surprised when the rumours get out of hand.

6.7 Prototype build

From the earliest days of getting the ITT/SOUR together, the team will have begun formulating ideas on how they are going to use the system and what it is going to do for the company. They will have refined these ideas during the demonstration phase and will have had those thoughts at the forefront of their minds when they had initial training from the system supplier. It is time now to build a prototype so that those ideas can be tested and, if necessary, adjusted. They need to perform a detailed 'gap analysis' to measure what the system can do against what they want and need it to do so that any remedial action can be planned, costed and, if appropriate, implemented.

Most systems come with a test area where daily running of the system can be simulated. In concert with your software supplier's consultants, this area should now be configured as closely as is possible to how it will be at go-live. Representative data should then be manually entered (we will consider data transfer later). With the exception of your financial chart of accounts, which needs to be complete so that your financial team can satisfy themselves that postings are going to the correct accounts, a cross section of your data will suffice.

Don't waste time entering all of your products, bills of material, customers, suppliers etc but do make sure that all bases are covered. If you buy and sell internationally, ensure that you have at least one foreign customer and supplier set up: this includes setting up currencies and rates of exchange. Don't just set up bills of materials for end items: ensure that products are set up with bills that extend down all levels to the purchased items even if you leave some components and sub-assemblies off.

The target is to enter enough data to enable you to do in the test system all that you would want and need to do in a live system but, if you can raise ten purchase orders, you can probably raise a thousand and, if you can invoice five foreign and five domestic customers, you can probably invoice five thousand so don't waste valuable time: apart from anything else, your tests might prompt you to do things differently and re-entering thousands of bills of material or customers is not a good use of time.

Why am I suggesting that you enter your test data manually? Partly because the routines necessary to transfer data from your old system may have to be written and tested, so you don't want to incur these costs until you are sure what you want to transfer and in what format. Additionally, after you have gone live, you will be manually entering new data regularly (customers, parts etc) so you need to get a feel for how this is done, how long it takes and what problems you might have. For example, data for the parts master file will come from several departments: can one department enter skeletal information and others chip in subsequently, or does some mandatory information, other than the part number, have to be entered just to allow a new part to be saved?

Having entered sufficient data, test everything that you would do in the system on a normal day. Your purpose is not to prove that the system works but to establish what it cannot do and under what circumstances using it becomes problematical. For example, most systems will allow purchase orders to be either manually entered or created electronically from MRP recommendations. If you decide that there are advantages to raising orders manually, don't just check that you can raise an order but also check how long it takes and then calculate the effort involved in raising a typical day's worth of orders. Likewise, closing an individual works order will be easy but calculate how many works orders you will need to transact daily and satisfy yourself that this is practical (see the comments on number of bills of material levels in section 4.6).

The test system is also the best place to develop and test workarounds and bespoke modifications. Remember that you will need a test system even after you have gone live to test new releases of the software and to test and evaluate changes as the system is changed to meet evolving business requirements. That means that you should not just throw it away after go-live but refresh it regularly by copying over your live system so that it is always representative of the way that the company is working.

When the prototype system is being tested, it should be tested by all of the team together as there are likely to be both new tasks and existing tasks that will change and, in doing so, beneficially move across departmental boundaries. For example, purchase receipting may move from the purchasing department to the warehouse and sales order invoicing may move from the finance department to the sales department. It is not enough to establish what has to be done: the team also has to establish the best person or department to do it.

All of these things need to be evaluated and agreed (in doing so, remember upward delegation). The team are the people best placed to make these judgements but, having done so, they should be documented and relayed via the project sponsor to all functional heads so that all necessary organisational adjustments can be carried out in an orderly fashion: neither senior management nor workers on the coal face enjoy last-minute surprises.

The project manager and the implementation team can expect to have to justify the changes that they propose but the expectation should be that, all having been selected by their heads of department, they will have the confidence of their managers and any head of department who rejects their conclusions should justify that withdrawal of support to the CEO. Obviously, if all team members have been working together and communicating continuously with their home departments, there should have been no surprises anyway.

Having received sign-off from senior management, the team must now document the new ways of working and write new procedures accordingly. This is an area where the team may not have the requisite skills and is an example of an instance when other specialists can be usefully co-opted onto the team for a specific task. Whilst doing this, they should not forget the value of training notes and 'crib sheets' that the users can have as comfort blankets at and immediately after go-live.

6.8 End-user training

You now have a signed-off prototype system in place. You have checked that it will do all that you need it to and any necessary workarounds have been developed and tested. It is time to roll training out to the end-users, remembering that their training needs are different from those of the implementation team. Whereas the implementation team need to know as close to everything as is possible, the end users just need to know what their role is in the new system and how to use it properly. To put it another way, the team needs to know how the software works but the users only need to know how to use it.

It is worth prefacing the user training sessions with an overview of how their bit of the system fits in with the company whole so that they understand the importance of getting things right and they can also see that, when a pebble is dropped in an integrated system, the ripples go a long way. One problem that is commonly faced in end-user training is that some users, for reasons that are discussed in the section 10.1.3, will turn up for training sessions with negative attitudes.

They will want to find fault in everything they see, whether to prove that it was a mistake not to have had them on the selection and implementation team or as a last ditch attempt to stop their world changing (see the discussion on 'Blue moons and red herrings' in section 10.2.3). Frequently they will turn up with calculators so that they can check all of the numbers. They will treat training as a software evaluation exercise and will delight in finding errors in test data, believing that they have found errors in the system. They will sow discord and, if allowed, they will erode enthusiasm and confidence in the system. Departmental managers must tell all their people, before training begins, that all functional heads have signed off the new system and obstruction in its implementation will not be tolerated or allowed. Rightly or wrongly, decisions have been made and a lot of money spent, so it is time for everyone to rally round and make a success of the new system for the company's sake.

On the other hand, there will also be users who want to learn more than you had intended to teach them. However well-meaning and enthusiastic, they can be disruptive by wanting to ask loads of questions during training sessions about functions or facilities that are not on the training schedule. To prevent this, the training session should be specific about what is being covered in each session and attendees told that, if it isn't in the schedule, it won't be covered. By all means, turn on extra training sessions if time allows, or allow users to attend sessions that border onto their area so that they can become 'super users', but avoid situations where the people being trained decide on what is to be taught. Believe me; if you have six people in a training session, you will have seven different opinions on what they need to know.

Again, a last thought: if the training is being carried out by your system supplier, it is of enormous benefit if at least one member of the implementation team sits in on every single training session and not just those covering their own area. In this way, there will be one coherent thread running through the entire process and it will be easier to re-tune training, perhaps in other areas, if unexpected points arise.

6.9 The Conference Room Pilot

This is so important that it really deserves a book on its own. However well the project has gone, it can fall at the last hurdle if the function of the conference room pilot (CRP) is not properly understood or it is not carried out properly. Ask people what a CRP is for and they will generally say that it is to test the system before it goes live but we need to define what we mean by 'the system'.

As we said very early on; MRPII is not a computer system: it is a people system that just happens to run on computers. The CRP, then, is as much about your people as it is about your software. Yes; you need to need to test that all of the programs are running successfully, that all new screens and reports are showing what they should, that all hardware from the network through to individual printers is functioning robustly, that all postings to your accounts are correct, and a host of other things. Only a properly planned and executed

CRP can do this, which is why I sometimes describe the process to people as being "a day in the life of" the company. Every last thing that will happen after go-live has to be tested before.

Which brings us to perhaps the most important point: to use another phrase, the CRP is a 'final dress rehearsal'. If it was for a stage play, you wouldn't have the author reading the lines and you wouldn't see the director striding the stage in a costume. Its purpose is not to check that things *can* work but to check that they *do* work. After go-live, everything will be done, not by the implementation team, but by the end users (the actors in our simile) so the CRP must test them also. If they are not ready, then the show cannot go on.

For a successful CRP, the implementation team must first have developed and published a detailed test plan and then they and the project manager should sit through the entire CRP process. It is also advisable to have consultants from the system supplier there in case something goes wrong but can be quickly fixed.

But most importantly, the project sponsor needs to be there and to be there all of the time. Knowing that they will be tested in front of a member of senior management will make it clear to everyone just how important the CRP is. If the CRP fails (and yes; they can and do fail) the project sponsor must be in no doubt as to why, because it will be the sponsor's responsibility (and not that of the project manager) to report that failure to the CEO and the rest of the senior management team. A CRP that takes between two and five days may seem to be an unwarranted use of executive time but remember that a company will typically spend between one and three per cent of its annual turnover on a new MRPII/ERP system and such expenditure surely demands and deserves their time. If you tell me that your sponsor cannot schedule a week into their diary, I'll ask what happens when they go on holiday or are taken ill. Does their department come to a stop then?

That then says that the purpose of the CRP is not to test the system before it goes live but to test the system to establish **whether or not** it can go live. And the people are the most important part of the system. There will, of course, be enormous pressure to take the system live. People will feel, quite rightly, that reputations depend on it and, regardless, having built up a head of steam, pulling the plug is a very serious and very visible thing to have to do. There will be a great temptation to view the results of the CRP through rose tinted glasses and assure everyone that individuals who did not display competence will be 'OK on the night'.

But ask yourself how they can be. If the reason for their failure is that they couldn't absorb the necessary training, what will be different the next time? If the reason was that they didn't take their training seriously, what will be different the next time? It is much easier to recover from a failed CRP than from a failed go–live so don't hesitate to put the brakes on if problems are apparent. And, if you have to put the project back following a failed CRP, make sure that you communicate the reasons to everyone in the company. If the reason is that bespoke modifications didn't work correctly, tell everyone. If the reason is that individuals or departments weren't ready, tell everyone. If you try to assuage people's feelings by saying that 'the system' wasn't ready, then don't be surprised when everyone loses faith in 'the system'.

Whatever you do, don't go live on the back of an unsuccessful CRP unless you really do believe in fairies.

6.10 Data Load

We have already discussed options for getting data into the new system (and see also the section on this in section 10.4 'What can go wrong?') but let's get into more detail.

As a rule of thumb, transferring static data (such as parts, customers etc) electronically between systems is relatively easy but transferring transactional data, such as histories, is infinitely more difficult. The reason is that data in customer and parts files, for example, tends not to differ wildly from system to system. In an integrated system, though, transactions can write to multiple files in complex structures. For example, a purchase receipt may write to a purchase order file, a stock file, a stock history file, the general ledger and may also write an accrual to the accounts payable file. In a relational database, these files will have automatically created indexes which would be painfully difficult to create manually.

6.10.1 Static data

When copying static data, your new system can be expected to have data fields that your old one didn't. These can be coped with, either by entering defaults, by manual intervention during the transfer or by mass updates afterwards (eg, if supplier is ABC, set purchase lead time to ten days: you get the idea). The main thing that you have to check is that field lengths are compatible; for example that you don't copy a 40 character part description to a 30 character field. Having copied data, the results must be conscientiously checked as, just because the routines finished without generating error messages doesn't necessarily mean that they worked correctly. I have seen such routines garble or lose data but still give the appearance of having been successful. So, before transferring data, every imaginable report must be run in the old system and, having been entered to the new system, every available report must be run there also. The two sets of reports must then be compared and anomalies investigated: near enough is not good enough.

6.10.2 Dynamic data

These fall into three categories; stock, financial and outstanding orders.

Stock balances

Some companies try to save time and effort by transferring stock balances from their old system. Except in the cases where they have been operating a cycle counting (perpetual inventory) system successfully for some time, the result is usually disastrous as they kick off a new system with inaccurate stock figures. As we discussed earlier on, MRP is pretty intolerant of inaccurate data and, when inaccurate MRP recommendations result, people generally blame 'the system', particularly if they have moved from manual systems where data could be easily interpreted. Unless you are totally confident in the accuracy of your stock figures, don't even think of entering them to the new system without having a full stock check first.

Financial data

On the financial side, it can be possible to transfer general ledger balances from your old system as long as the chart of accounts structure has not been radically altered. Many financial departments will, however, have taken advantage of additional features in the new system by amending the account code structure so it may be necessary to raise manual journals to get the data in.

When it comes to loading outstanding accounts payable and accounts receivable invoices, companies take one of three paths. At one extreme, if the number of invoices is not great, it can be viable to manually recreate them in the new system, whilst if the number is great, some companies will create summary invoices; one for each customer and supplier with just one consolidated total. My preferred option is to enter a summary invoice for each customer and supplier at month or period level so that, for example, sensible aged debt reports can continue to be run. On the accounts payable side, this also makes it a lot easier to ensure that you continue to pay invoices on-time and not un-necessarily early or dangerously late.

Outstanding orders

Let's consider sales and purchase orders first. Again; these cannot easily be transferred electronically from your old systems because of differing file structures and there will frequently be doubts about their accuracy as well. Keying them manually to the new system may be onerous but at least you will know that you are not transferring garbage. In entering such orders, time is on your side however, as there will generally be a period of weeks between loading the new software and going live. It should be easy to give end users training in order entry (only) quite early in the implementation. Then they can work through the outstanding orders and enter to the new system only those that are due for delivery after the planned go-live date.

Obviously there can be orders delivered early or late so this exercise cannot be 100% accurate and some adjustment will be necessary immediately prior to go-live but, in addition to ensuring that your files are accurate, it has the considerable benefit of giving your people useful practice in order entry so that, at go-live, they will be more confident and pressures on them, and the implementation team members who will be supporting them in the early days, will be reduced.

Entering outstanding works orders is a rather more complex operation for most companies. If you have short manufacturing lead times you can return un-used components to stock (not physically), close out the old works orders and raise new ones for the outstanding balances. The main problem that you will have is if you have a lot of works orders in progress as you can't do this until immediately prior to go-live.

However, if you have long manufacturing lead times, you have a bigger problem. If you have short lead times, you are generally making large quantities of items, so closing a works order short is not a problem but, if you have long manufacturing lead times, you will typically be manufacturing in small numbers. If you are making, say, one large item, you can't complete half an item to stock. You can close the old order with a zero completion quantity and then continue with a new order but this is going to mess up your costs, so let's look at your options.

Firstly, some systems will let you enter negative transactions, so you could reverse all of the material, labour and overhead postings and then re-transact these in the new system. This means putting WIP components back into stock so be careful that you co-ordinate this with your go-live stock take as, depending on your timing, the new system will show stock that is not actually in the warehouse and will not be counted there. Frequently it is necessary to enter your stock count, add on your WIP components and then issue your new works orders. Re-entering labour transactions to new orders is generally easier because there are no balances to consider but do ensure that, at a financial level, everyone is comfortable that, in the go-live month, you may have an over-recovery on your labour and overhead accounts.

In some companies, the above methodologies may be impractical but you still need to get accurate WIP cost figures into your new system if only to ensure that your cost of sale or manufacturing variance figures are accurate. Some systems allow 'miscellaneous' costs to be added and, if your new system does, it can be viable to load costs at a summary level, even if adjustment details need to be manually journalled to the general ledger subsequently.

Transaction history

As with other data that we have discussed, differing file structures in your old and new systems usually make it very difficult (i.e. prohibitively expensive) to transfer transaction history, although some systems will offer facilities for some data to be entered at a summary level. You may be able to get data out of your old system and into spreadsheets but that will depend on someone in the company having a good understanding of its file structures. Regardless; unless you have money to burn, don't even think of transferring it into your new system, even if the alternatives is to produce a load of hard copy reports and store them at the back of the warehouse.

7. Go-live

F irst of all: timing. The go-live date may have been forced on you by another event, such as a new financial year or the withdrawal of support for the old system but avoid if you can going live after a long factory shutdown, such as a holiday closure. Users must have been encouraged to practice their new skills between training and go-live so that they don't get rusty, but even a couple of weeks away from new screens has a marked effect on competence in the early days.

Before going live with the new system, some things are essential and are non-negotiable:

- You must have completed a successful conference room pilot (CRP), in which all software, hardware, documentation and people performed faultlessly. Going live with the belief that 'everything will be OK on the night' is unprofessional and dangerous.
- All data must have been entered, checked and verified.
- All department heads must have visibly and loudly nailed their colours to the new system mast. Any hesitation, equivocation or caveats will weaken the resolve of their staff to persevere if teething troubles occur.
- Following on from that, everyone must be told that teething problems will indeed occur. People will make mistakes,

checked data will turn out not to have been checked properly and, at some point, Murphy's Law will kick in. People must be told this and be told what contingency plans are in place to cope (reverting to the old system is not a contingency plan and should be explicitly ruled out).

Some things are not mandatory but can be useful:

- If customer and supplier facing documents such as purchase orders, invoices etc, are dramatically changing, it can be a good idea to let key trading partners see examples (clearly marked 'SAMPLE'!) in advance.
- Likewise, it can be helpful to write to both customers and suppliers, advising them that you are moving to a new system and requesting their patience and forbearance should anything go wrong and they be affected.
- Lastly, there will be go-live nerves amongst the users. Giving them simple 'crib sheets', that walk them through the things they will be doing, greatly increases their confidence in being able to cope. (Such documents are also very useful later, when people are off ill or on holiday).

It is worth remembering that, when things go wrong, the system will be blamed and, by inference, the implementation team. It is useful to remind them that the users have had training and that the data both belongs to the users and has been checked by them. The vast majority of problems at go-live are user problems and, though the implementation team are essential to resolving problems, they should not feel responsible for those problems. This also means that, when problems occur, the reasons for them must be communicated to everyone. If it genuinely is a system problem, then everyone should be told. But, if is a people problem, everyone must also be told. If you try to assuage people's feelings, 'the system' will take the blame for their failings and, if you allow that to happen, don't be surprised when people lose faith and revert to note pads and spreadsheets.

Also be aware that, at go-live, you will find that it takes longer to correct mistakes that make mistakes. For that reason, you need as many hands on deck as you can possibly get and that includes the consultants from your system supplier. Some companies try to save money by avoiding this, and it is undeniably painful to see expensive consultants sitting around drinking coffee with nothing to do (surely you can find them something?), but believe me, there are times in life when you can do without insurance and this is not one of them.

8.   Post go-live

You have successfully gone live and any initial teething problems have been overcome. Time to pack up the team; right?

No: the team still has vital roles to play. Firstly, following go-live, the users should be encouraged to write down all niggles and problems they are having with the new system. The implementation team will be capable of resolving a lot of these but, after one month, three months and twelve months, you external consultants should be invited back to discuss those outstanding. As an implementation consultant I was always saddened when, months or even years after go-live, I visited companies that avoided the 'expense' of these reviews and found that they had been limping along with problems and irritants that took minutes to fix. The users must, of course, be told that not all of their problems can be resolved but I used to say to clients that, whilst I could not guarantee that any problem they reported would get fixed, I could guarantee that any problem that didn't get reported would not get fixed.

In the original justification for the new system, measurable targets will have been set for things such as inventory reduction, service level improvement, reduction in debtor days etc. The team should continually monitor performance against these targets. If expectations are not being met, the team must, perhaps with the assistance of the external consultants, find out what areas of the system are under performing and must deliver plans for remedial action. On the other hand, if the system is meeting or surpassing expectations, everyone in the company must be told. The more they are told that the system is working, the more they will have confidence in it, and the more they have confidence in it, the better they will use it.

The company should also get details of any user groups from their system supplier and the team should maintain contact with such groups so that the company can benefit from other people's experiences. Lastly, they should try to maintain informal contact with the implementation consultants. Giving away free consultancy will not be in their remit but most will be happy to answer brief questions over the phone or via e-mail.

9. And finally

You now have a team of people who know the company and its systems better that you could ever have imagined. Use them. Use them to monitor changes in the company and the way that it operates so that the system can be continuously re-tuned to meet developing business requirements. Use them to review radical changes, such as acquisitions or new product lines, so that effects on the system, or ways in which the system might help, can be evaluated. Use them to continually look at new and potentially better ways of doing things.

You have invested time and money in your new system: now is the time to reap the rewards.

10. What can go wrong?

Those of you who have read this far will have realised that I believe in MRPII. I know that, properly implemented, it works and it profoundly changes companies and the way they operate. That then gave me a dilemma when it came to writing this chapter because, for those whose commitment to implementing MRPII is less than total, I will potentially be providing many reasons not to go ahead. Should I do something that might dissuade you from doing something that could transform your company and turn it from an also-ran to an industry leader?

The answer is that I should. No MRPII implementation was ever successful when it was not driven with commitment and belief. Half-hearted implementations fail. If you have doubts about whether MRPII is for you; if you have doubts about your company's ability to embrace new concepts, then stop now. If the project goes on hold, you can resurrect it at some point in the future (assuming that you are still in business) but, if you try and you fail, you will find it immensely difficult to gather support and confidence for a second attempt. In the eyes of the company, it will have been proven that all the horror stories about MRPII were true; that it doesn't work and can't be made to work. Yes; you can with great difficulty turn things around and failed implementations can and have been rescued but it takes more time, more money and more energy that if things had been done properly in the first place.

But enough of the pessimism. This chapter was written in the belief that forewarned is forearmed; that all of the problems that you may hit have been encountered before and that solutions to all of them have been developed over many years of successful implementations. In going down the MRPII route, you are travelling a well-trodden path and all you need to ensure that you do not go astray is to plan your route properly and to take advantage of any guides who are available and who have demonstrated that they know the way.

So let's look at the problems that you might encounter and what can be done about them. Some of these will have been discussed earlier but it will do no harm to consider them again. For ease of reference, I am going to split the problems into four categories: people, systems, planning and data.

10.1 People

It is no coincidence that, when writing that last sentence, people were at the forefront of my mind. As we said earlier, MRPII is not a computer system; it is a people system that just happens to run on computers. So let's look at people problems first.

10.1.1 The role of the project sponsor is sometimes not correctly understood.

We have seen that the roles of project sponsor and project manager must be fulfilled by people who have respect from all departments and who, regardless of their background and line responsibilities, simply must be seen to be dealing even-handedly with all individuals and departments involved in the implementation. Their neutrality in any debate or conflict must be without question, as any statements or actions that are seen to be partisan will destroy the unity of the team. It will then be believed that the new system is being weighted unfairly towards a particular department and people do not like being treated unfairly. Their commitment, enthusiasm and support will disappear overnight and their disenchantment will find its way back to their home departments. The project sponsor and the project manager must have the confidence of the team they lead and they can only keep that confidence by communicating openly, honestly and constantly. When decisions go in their departments' favour, they must be especially careful to explain the thought processes behind those decisions.

Some project sponsors lose control of the project because they do not understand their role. They see it as being reactive; a figurehead role and almost symbolic in nature. This is most certainly not the case. Whilst the project manager must manage the implementation, the project sponsor must lead it, and leadership must be proactive. The team needs to be guided, counselled and, perhaps more than anything, inspired by the project sponsor. If problems mount and morale drops, the project sponsor must rally the troops and get the enthusiasm pumping again. Although the sponsor must be careful not to upstage the project manager, if he or she waits until something goes wrong before involving themselves, the project will suffer. Project sponsors who prevent their teams walking into minefields are more valuable than those who can lead them out.

One last thought on how project sponsors lose control of the project by being reactive. In terms of expenditure, the project is quite possibly the biggest thing to hit your company in years. A lot of people will see advantage in linking smaller projects to the MRPII project in the belief, or at least hope, that they can get the necessary budget signed off under that larger banner. One way to do this is to expand the scope of the project so that, for example, bar-coding becomes 'essential', or a particular department finds that they need to upgrade all of their PCs and printers. I once saw a design department sneak a new CAD server onto an MRPII budget. Where was the project sponsor when that happened?

10.1.2 Star players are omitted from the team.

We have also previously highlighted the total necessity of the selection and implementation team being the best of your people and not the most expendable. These people will be laying a course that will be followed by the company for years to come. Micro-managing second-raters simply does not work. You may feel that it is impossible to be without your best people but what would you do if they walked under a bus tomorrow? What would you do if, having seen a lesser talent entrusted with the department's future, they upped and left? Use your best people for the most important jobs.

10.1.3 Internal sabotage.

Harsh words, but resistance to the new system can start when people are excluded from the selection and implementation team. People can feel slighted; especially if they are experienced and long term employees. What you cannot afford to do is to try to soften that disappointment by leading people to believe that they will have an influence over proceedings, when they won't, and perhaps even a right of veto when decisions are taken, when they can't.

It is not possible for everyone to be involved in the process and, if people are allowed or encouraged to believe something that doesn't subsequently happen, they will feel cheated. There will however, during the life of the project, be occasions when extra members need to be co-opted onto the team to carry out specific tasks for a finite amount of time. This can open up opportunities for other people to contribute as long as it is made clear to them that their role will be restricted to tasks delegated to them by the team, who will retain authority throughout.

Departmental managers must explain the process to their own staff members and must also explain why their departmental representative was chosen. Staff should be told that they have an important role to play in supporting that representative and reassured that, whilst it is impossible for everyone to take part in decisions, their wants and needs will be listened to. They should, however, be reminded that packaged systems involve compromises, and perfect systems do not exist; so some people, some times, will not get all that they ask for. If managers do not have the confidence and trust of their staff, that needs to be addressed but it is not a system issue and cannot be covered here.

Many promising implementations have been sabotaged from within; sometimes by implementation members who rejected the team ethos, sometimes by heads of departments who were not getting their way, and sometimes by whole departments who felt that they lost out during the selection phase. In all good organisations, all departments should be equal but, in many companies, some departments see themselves as being 'more equal' than others. They will be shocked that others in the organisation cannot see how their department's requirements must be paramount and that they have, as a result, made a selection that they view to be nothing less than stupid. They can then devote such time to 'proving' that the new system 'does not work' that, had the same degree of effort been applied to finding ways that the system *could* work, the success of the project would be have been assured.

The project manager must advise the project sponsor when support is being withheld or when obstacles are being put in the way of success. If the problems cannot be resolved at departmental manager level, they must be escalated to the very highest level of management immediately. No one individual or even department can be allowed to be bigger than the company itself. When an expensive project is being jeopardised, there comes a point when managers or the CEO have to show people the door.

Fear of the unknown can also cause people to fight against a new system. So what can you do to alleviate this? Start with open and honest communication. The project sponsor must tell everyone who will be using the system, or will be affected by it, what is going to happen, and why. This may take the form of departmental meetings that the project sponsor addresses, although, in larger companies, it may be necessary for him or her to address managers and supervisors and for those people to pass on the news to their own staff. This can be backed up by a newsletter from the project sponsor so that everyone can see that the project is being led from the very top.

People need to be told why the decision has been taken to implement a company-wide system. They need to know, and understand, that the search will be for a system that benefits the company as a whole, and not just individual departments, and they then need to know and understand that this will involve compromise. It is time also to start addressing the other fears that are risks to projects; the fear of not being able to cope with a new system and the fear that jobs will go. Let's think about those two fears for a moment.

However bad your current system, there will be people who are comfortable with it. They know their way around it and how to deal with its shortcomings. They may even enjoy a status of being people who can make it work as best it can, and people to be consulted and asked for advice when things go wrong. You are about to take that away from them and put them back at the beginning of the learning curve where everyone becomes equal. In terms of the system, you will be asking some of your most experienced and valuable people to start again. Sadly, there is another factor to consider. If your current system is seen as being weak or poor, people have a ready excuse for doing a second rate job: a new system may well expose them. No wonder they are frightened.

There is no doubt that a good system will shine light into dark corners. Comfort blankets will be taken away and people who were enjoying expert status will have to earn their spurs again. One thing that we can do is remind people how they came to be regarded as experts in the first place. It was probably because of their knowledge of the company and how it works (qualities that will again be needed when the new system comes in) and their ability to both learn and to pass on that learning. When you actually implement the system, there will be a need for departmental and section 'super users'. Don't hand out these roles like confetti but remember that tried and trusted staff who might otherwise doubt their ability to cope will welcome both the status and the extra training that such positions offer.

Fear of losing jobs is commonplace, even when job cuts are not a stated reason for bringing in a new system. But here is an interesting fact: in over twenty years' experience of implementing MRPII systems, I have never seen a well-implemented system result in job losses. Note though that I said 'well-implemented'—I have seen many badly implemented systems result in job losses when the company makes such a mess of it that it loses competitiveness and maybe even goes out of business. In truth, most of these companies were so badly run that they would have gone out of business in time anyway (if you don't have the skills to implement an MRPII system, you don't have the skills to run a company).

Here is another fact: my experience is that many companies that successfully implement MRPII in fact do the very opposite of laying-off staff. They find that, because they are a more efficient and effective organisation, they do more business and doing more business grows the company and calls for more staff.

10.1.4 The team fails to be a team.

Teamwork can be difficult for some people who are used to working on their own. What can happen then is that they try to work independently of the other members in the belief that, when they deliver their part of the project, it can be fitted in with the rest seamlessly. Company wide systems are, unfortunately, just that. From any one area, tentacles reach out into others and actions or inactions in one area can cause ripples in many. We need these people to understand this and to understand also that a successful team is greater than the sum of its parts. Everyone on the team can help with all of the problems that the team faces. Individuals who try to operate independently deny themselves and other team members that support.

Additionally, whatever debate and dispute goes on within the team, they must present a united front to the rest of the world. That means that they must know what each other is doing and why it is being done. When people do not work as part of the team, they can't know those things and they can't feed back to their own department's positive and encouraging news about the progress being made. Confidence then fades.

However, for the team to come together and gel, all members must be comfortable with working together and must regard each other as equals. It is difficult for this to be the case if they come from differing levels within the organisation so the dynamics of the team must be considered when it is put together so that artificial frictions are not generated. Provision of a dedicated project room helps engender a team identity and, with that, a team spirit. On even the smallest project in the smallest company, the team must have a 'home'. If you still can't get everyone pulling together, and sending them on a team–building activity doesn't work either, you are going to have to bite the bullet and remove offenders from the team, regardless of value.

10.1.5 External consultants can have an undue influence.

We have already noted that the project will need a guide who has travelled the route before (the more times the better) but sometimes those consultants will have their own agenda. When involved in the selection process, their advice can be biased towards a particular package or provider for reasons of commercial advantage (to them). They can usefully tell you how to select a package but should not be allowed to select it for you. They can usefully tell you what decisions you have to take but should not be allowed to make those decisions. They can help you run the project but should not run the project themselves. Use them with caution and make sure you know whose side they are on. They have a responsibility to their own organisation to make money but they also have a responsibility to your organisation to offer advice that is genuinely impartial.

One last thought about consultants. When everyone is busy running the business, it sometimes seems easier to sit back and let the consultants do all of the work. This causes two problems: firstly that the system is then seen as the consultants' system and people are slow to take ownership. Secondly, and perhaps more damagingly, when the consultants leave at the end of the project they will take with them the knowledge of your system and how it works. Systems need to regularly re-tuned to their environment as the business changes and, if the only people who know enough to achieve this are external consultants who took the knowledge with them when they left, there is a real danger that the job will not get done. After a year or two, getting back the same people who worked with you on the original implementation is not always possible and it is, anyway, an expensive route to go down for the minor tweaks that can be called for and which can make a big difference to the smooth running and continued success of the system. Whenever possible, keep whatever expertise you have expensively acquired in-house.

10.1.6 Inappropriate cost cutting.

ERP/MRPII systems are expensive. They are expensive to buy and expensive to implement. Before committing yourself to that expenditure you will have been through a cost justification exercise (won't you?). Nevertheless, when the bills start to roll in, more than a few companies try to find ways of cutting costs especially when things like mission creep start to escalate them. They can't at this stage cut costs on software (apart from bespoke) so the only places where cuts can have any real effect are in consultancy and training. Both are expensive (although you will have heard the expression, "If you think training is expensive, try ignorance") but let's look at the damage cost cuts here can cause.

Cutting back on training is like buying a BMW and never taking it out of first gear. You will drive it knowing that it can perform better but you won't know what to do about it. You will spend time and money on developing clumsy and unnecessary work-arounds, you will drift back to spreadsheets and notebooks and everyone will view the new system as a disappointing waste of money. And it will have been. Going back to the BMW analogy, you wouldn't give the keys to a new car to someone who had never driven before and ask them to teach themselves to drive in it. Whether you are driving a car or a computer system, learning to drive needs time and tuition.

Consultancy is sometimes so close to training that it is hard to draw a line between the two. In all but the simplest systems, there will be more than one way of doing most things. Without consultancy, what is the person responsible for delivering the training to do? It is probably wasteful to go into any detail on options that you will not use and which are inappropriate to the way your company works. Frequently there will be choices that conflict but you can't expect a consultant or trainer who has spent a long time learning a system, and the best way to use it in different circumstances, to be able to pass all of that knowledge over to you in a day, a week or a month. It is just not possible.

What happens when there is insufficient training time is that someone has to decide on what doesn't get taught and what gets skimped. Who is best placed to make that decision; a system supplier who doesn't know your business or your people who don't what the system can do? Frequently the customer chooses a compromise: training is done by question and answer. Is that how you learned at school? Could I have learnt algebra by asking my teacher loads of questions? No; and for good reason—the results are disastrous.

As a rule of thumb, the amount of money that you spend on training and consultancy on a successful implementation will be about the same as you spent on the software. If you are happy with an unsuccessful implementation, go for less.

10.1.7 Panic.

Things go wrong during system implementations. However well you have planned it, surprises happen: people leave the company, the company changes direction, things that you thought were going to work don't. When everybody is geared up and excited about a project, unexpected reversals can damage confidence to the extent that very promising implementations can be halted for very little reason and, as we said earlier, if a project comes to a halt it can be very difficult to get it going again. But sometimes the panic kicks in after a good project has gone live when people don't understand what is happening and assume the worst. Let me explain.

We have all read the books and we have all been on the courses so we know that, when you switch on a good MRPII system, stock levels fall; don't they? No! In all probability they will rise: but don't panic. When I explain why, you will not only understand, but you will know something that no book or course that I have ever been on told me.

In this book, we have used the word 'stock' a number of times but there are actually different kinds of stock. There is stock that we have that we need; there is stock that we have that we don't need, and there is stock that we need that we don't have. When you switch on a good MRPII system for the first time, the MRP module may well recognise that you have excessive stocks of some items but, apart from telling you not to order any more, it can do nothing about it. But it may also recognise shortages on other items and, correctly, advise replenishment. The result is that your shortages come in but your excesses remain and overall stock levels rise.

Now; over a period of time, your excess stocks dwindle and, allied to the improved stock efficiency that you get with MRP, stock levels fall and continue to fall until the books and courses are right and your stock levels are markedly less than they were before implementation. Nevertheless, you can't avoid that initial blip. There are two questions that you will want to ask: how big is that blip and how long will it last?

The main factor in answering these questions is how long your purchase lead times are. If you have long lead times on items that you have shortages for, the stock level rise can go on for some time. At the same time, though, your excess stocks will be eaten into by regular demand (unless they are obsolete stocks). If you were to draw these two occurrences on a graph, the rising line showing shortages will at some point cross the excess stock line coming down but I can't give you a formula to calculate that point because neither line is likely to be straight. The maximum increase in stock value that you can get can be measured by costing all of your shortages at go-live, and the maximum amount of time that it will continue will be the maximum purchase lead time that you have although, obviously, both of these are maximums and unlikely to be reached.

The important thing is that you understand what is going to happen and that you warn anyone who doesn't. Finance departments and warehouse managers can, in particular, get nervous when stock levels seem to be running away with themselves. Explain the phenomenon and they won't panic.

10.2 Systems

There is no doubt that a bad system implemented well will outperform a good system that is implemented badly. Notwithstanding that, avoidable mistakes can be made.

10.2.1 Inappropriate system selected.

We debated this previously in chapter 5 but let's remind ourselves that MRP is an irrelevance in some manufacturing companies, such as job shops and companies with very simple materials management requirements. It may be that their overall business requirements are such that the best answer is to buy an ERP/MRPII system to handle sales, purchasing, stock control and finance and then to simply switch off the MRP module, but what they should never do is to try to use inappropriate functionality just because it is there.

10.2.2 Contract MRP.

Contract MRP (or Project MRP) is a dinosaur that has somehow not quite become extinct. It could have been part of the previous section (Inappropriate systems) but, because of the damage that it can do, I thought it worthy of a spot on its own. It is such an outdated concept that many of you will not have heard about it so I'll start with a quick summary of what it is and what it tries to do.

Contract MRP came from a background of companies in a make-to-order environment and the companies who adopted it were frequently those who operated in a 'cost-plus' market, usually in the engineering field. Cost-plus manufacture was a way of coping with uncertain research and development (R&D) costs in major government contracts in areas such as aerospace which were pushing at the leading edge of technology. It was almost impossible for companies to estimate accurately for jobs where new technology was required and was perhaps still being developed, so the idea of paying companies a percentage on top of their costs seemed a pragmatic way of ensuring that the leading edge didn't become the bleeding edge and they were not put off bidding for work by uncertain costs.

The downside of the concept is that, though it allowed technology to progress, it did nothing to encourage manufacturers to drive down costs or to become more efficient. There were different types of cost-plus arrangement; the worst of which paid manufacturers an agreed percentage profit on top of their costs. Reasonable though this may sound (it seems to offer a way of preventing excessive profits), it actually meant that companies could increase their profits by increasing their costs! Ironically, the less efficient you became, the more money you made. This encouraged working practices and mind-sets that did untold damage to industry (and the customer)—witness the UK Government's recent Nimrod MR2 reconnaissance aircraft fiasco.

One feature of cost-plus was that, in order to ensure that companies were not destroyed by cash flow over multi-year projects, companies could invoice the Government for costs as soon as they were incurred (and, in doing so, earn their profit on those costs). That encouraged companies to order, and take delivery of, materials as soon as they possibly could and not to wait for when those materials were actually needed. In order to do this as quickly as possible, opportunities for consolidating requirements were ignored; indeed they were actively avoided as they might have reduced costs had they resulted in quantity discounts!

Now that we know what it is, let's consider how it works. When a new contract is entered to the system, the users want to immediately know all of the items that need to be purchased. Some low value items may be bought in bulk but most items will be bought for each order separately so there will be no consolidation of requirements. Each purchase order will be for a specific contract and that contract number will be held on the order so that, when the items are delivered, they can be immediately allocated to that contract. Frequently there will be a marshalling area for each contract so the items will not go into a general storage area.

The thinking behind this way of working is that:

- At any one time, you can see what has been ordered for a contract, what has been delivered and what is short.
- Because materials do not go into a general stock but are put immediately into a contract-specific marshalling area, they are handled once and not twice.

The logic is that materials 'belong' to a specific contract from the minute that they are ordered.

This of course becomes a nonsense the moment one of your suppliers is late or short-delivers an item that is used on multiple contracts. At that stage, your supplier will deliver against the earliest purchase order, which may well not be for your most important order or customer. At that stage, even devoted adherents of contract MRP admit that they cannot afford to let suppliers decide their priorities and that they will happily 'rob' contracts. The administration costs of managing this are conveniently forgotten.

The argument that materials are only handled once is similarly flawed: unless you have enough space in production areas for all materials to be held there (and who does nowadays?) the materials will still have to be moved from the contract marshalling area to the point of use.

Very few companies use contract MRP because most of those who refused to move from such inefficient methods have not survived. I did try to find such a system for a client that insisted that they needed it but not even Mr Google could help me. It is also worth noting that, when they requested my assistance, they were, as a business, less than a quarter of the size they were just four or five years previously. Will they survive another four or five years? I think not. To be inefficient today is a major problem but to be intentionally inefficient is almost suicidal.

10.2.3 Blue moons and red herrings.

Before you begin to select a system, you will draw up a document (ITT/SOUR) that specifies the business problems that the system is required to address. When asked what our biggest and most serious problems are, it is natural to think of the problems that have occurred most recently or which have caused the biggest problem. It is difficult to be truly objective. The problem that caused us a real headache yesterday might not occur again for months, if at all, but the pain that we feel today is not something that we want to feel again. For that reason, we will want the new system to provide a means of avoiding that problem in the future.

But you can't build a system around exceptions; the things that happen once in a blue moon. Exceptions should be dealt with exceptionally, and a well implemented system facilitates this by handling the routine things routinely. No system can replace the Mark 1 Human Brain for coping with the unexpected. All that systems can do is to free-up people's time so that exceptions can be managed more effectively. Remember: in the words of Confucius, the best is the enemy of the good. Or, to put it another way, if you try to build a system that tries to do everything, you'll end up with a system that never gets completed.

Turning our attention to red herrings, where do these come from? All of us have elements of our jobs that we do not like and would happily relinquish. When you are gathering requirements for the ITT/SOUR, some people will see opportunities for the bits of their jobs that they don't like to be stripped out and given to someone else. They will exaggerate problems that do exist and invent others that do not. An advantage of having a team approach to selection and implementation is that these falsities stand a much better chance of being identified for what they are.

You should also never underestimate the desire for people in mundane jobs to see their names up in lights occasionally and to feel important. They will exaggerate the importance of what they do and will see it as imperative that the new system addresses these areas. Without doubt, in your company today, there are people doing things that need not, indeed should not, be done. In one implementation, an accounts clerk said how important it was for her to monitor currency exchange rates daily and to enter them to a spreadsheet. She asked how this would be managed in the new system. Her justification for performing this task daily was that it was important information and it would be embarrassing for the department if anyone ever asked for it and they didn't have it. It wasn't important and no-one ever asked for it.

10.2.4 Black magic

No; I don't mean that someone will put a curse on your system. I mean that some systems can be too clever for their own good and, if people don't understand how they work, they will not trust them or their output. In researching some things for this book, I checked on the Wagner-Within Algorithm for EOQ calculation but the website that advocated its use warned me that I would be very unlikely to understand how it works. Am I likely then to trust it? No. Am I likely then to use it? Again, no. Those of us, who have been around MRP for some time, know how it works and can therefore trust it but it is easy to forget that some of our colleagues don't have that advantage. They feel that they are shovelling data into a black hole and being asked to trust and to react to messages that mysteriously appear.

The answer is that those of us who are clever need to be a little less clever; or at least that we should share our knowledge. We should take the time and trouble to explain to everybody in the company how MRP works. If you don't feel comfortable about standing up in front of a room full of people, you should ask a consultant to do it for you. This has the added advantage of testing the consultant's knowledge: if they ask for time to prepare a presentation, they don't know MRP.

Yes, it is nice to have the time to put together a bespoke presentation but, if a consultant can't stand in front of a white board at zero notice and explain MRP, then they really don't know it. Trust me: I've done it. Remember also that R J Mitchell, who designed the Spitfire, said in the nineteen thirties that, if you truly understand something, you can explain it to your gardener. Granted, that was before the era of TV and celebrity millionaire gardeners, but you get my point. A friend of mine once explained Einstein's Theory of Relativity to me and made it sound simple. He could do that because he knew and understood it. Anyone who can't make MRP sound simple is telling you something!

10.2.5 Reinventing the wheel

When you set off to select a new system, there is always the temptation to use your present system as a template and just look for a system that just plugs perceived gaps. We have already noted in the Selection chapter that this can be dangerous; as we cannot assume that any new system does all that the old system did, even if it comes from the same supplier. Different systems have different design teams and these teams will have differing views on what is required in a system. There is also the common danger that a lot of money was spent on bespoke modifications for your old system and what you now think of as being a standard system is not standard at all.

Throw in resistance to change and you can easily end up with a new system that is no better than the old one. It might have a new user interface and nicer screens, and it might not crash as often as the old one, but you haven't moved forward. A new system means and needs change. To the people who say, "I want everything to be different but nothing to change", I would reply with what an old-timer said to me years ago: "If you always do what you've always done, you'll always get what you've always had".

But, again, help is at hand from your contacts and trading partners. Many will be willing to host visits from your team to discuss their systems and the way they work. That can expose the team to new ways of doing things and new ways of thinking about problems, and frequently has the added benefit of strengthening relationships with those partners.

Remember not to look for a system that fits what you are doing now: look for one that fits where you want the company to be tomorrow.

10.2.6 Too much bespoke.

This problem can be related to the previous one in that they both try to limit change; be that change in the way the company works or change in the way that individuals work. It can also be caused by people conscientiously striving for the best system possible but, in the words of Confucius, "The best is the enemy of the good".

Here's an interesting fact: typically, three years into live running of a system, less than 30% of the bespoke software written for it is still in use. In fact, frequently it never gets used at all. But the writing of that bespoke added unnecessary cost to the project and probably delayed it. Too much delay and too much cost and sometimes senior management either pulls the plug on the project or takes a decision to go-live without the specified modifications being completed. The phrase, "We've spent enough!" can be heard. You then either go live with a system that has un-planned holes in it or, sometimes, senior management gets so bored or frustrated with the project that you don't go live at all.

Remember that bespoke software has a continuing cost over the years that the software will be in use (hopefully at least ten). There is the initial cost of writing it, there is the cost of modifying it every time the system authors issue a new release of the package and, potentially, there is the cost of not being able to move to a new release at all because the cost of re-writing modifications is prohibitive. Packaged software is written to be flexible but bespoke software generally is not, so you can find yourself with a system that is stuck in a time warp whilst the company and the core package move ahead.

10.2.7 Too much data!

I sometimes think that the end of the world will be caused by the laser printer. It is so easy to generate and print enormous reports nowadays that I suspect that some people see a 500-page MRP recommendations report as an achievement. "Look at all that data! Wow!" But data is not information and information is not knowledge. I have seen good people take early retirement when bombarded with more data they can process. If you have generated a 500-page MRP report, the chances are that, unless you are an enormous company with teams of buyers and planners, you have generated more information than can be processed.

Take a look at that report again. How many of the actions that it recommends are in fact trivial? Is it asking you to push back low-value purchase orders by a matter of days? Is it asking you to amend order quantities for washers and screws? Whilst you sort through the trivia, are you neglecting to do the important things that will keep the production line running?

Probably you are. We have already noted that consumables can be handled efficiently and cheaply outside of the MRP system but it is time now to look at the messages that we are likely to get from MRP. If a sane and sensible person would not react to them, they should not be on the report. To the person who wants to look at a report and see everything, I would say, "Read that last sentence again".

10.2.8 Because it was there

We have all heard of the mountaineer's reply when asked why they climbed a mountain, "Because it was there". A similar reply is often given to a question about why a particular piece of system functionality was switched on, or why a particular field on a database was populated.

But don't put all of your parts under MRP control just because you can. Don't build 99-level bills of material just because the system supports them. In short; don't do anything 'just because'.

10.3 Planning

10.3.1 No change management

We have mentioned a couple of times before the danger of 'mission creep'. You set out to deliver what was specified in the ITT/SOUR but more and more creeps in. Talk to any experienced software implementation consultant and they will tell you that, whilst on customer sites, the most common phrases that they hear begin with, "Whilst you are here," and "Can you also just". During the implementation phase, there will be dozens of good reasons why extra functionality should be turned on and extra reports written. But it is essential that these are handled by a formal change management system so that their impact on project timescales and budgets can be properly assessed before expensive programmers and consultants go to work on things that might even conflict with other areas of the system. When the system is late and over budget, everyone will have forgotten the reasons why.

10.3.2 Unrealistic timescales

When you don't regularly implement MRPII systems it can be very easy to under-estimate the amount of time required. Even when implementing sizeable systems I have come across people who like a 'unit of measure' of a week. So they plan for one week to load the software, another week to load the data and another week to train all of the users; then go-live on week four. I remember telling one CEO that such timescales were unrealistic and he responded by telling me that, when they last implemented a system, they were up and running in a few weeks. When I asked what system that was, he replied with the name of a spreadsheet package!

Excellent software though that particular package might have been, MRPII is not a spreadsheet. Hopefully by the time you have got to this point in the book you will have agreed that a successful implementation takes time. Chapter 6, on implementation, details all of the things that have to be done and gives an idea of how long they take. Even for a small system, anything less than three months is pushing your luck. For medium sized systems, think six to nine months and for the large heavyweights think two years. Yes they can be done faster if you throw money at them but not much faster.

Good implementations take time: time to plan, time to work out how best to use any new features or functionality, time to develop work-arounds for things that the system can't do, time to get the data right, time to properly train people and time to properly test the system before go-live. But not too much time. Taking too much time is not as bad as taking too little but be aware that it also causes problems. On a long project, people can get tired and perhaps bored when they start to miss their regular jobs. Some people may even move on and we have mentioned before the difficulty of grafting in replacements during a project. Be realistic in your planning: as you put together a detailed plan, you will get a feel for how much work has to be done and always remember that there is an awful lot of free advice out there if you just ask for it.

10.3.3 Underestimating the task.

To an extent, we have covered this above but it is worth a section of its own. Selecting and implementing a system, especially a small system, can seem like a small task. We related above how timescales can be unrealistic and how there can be a temptation not to use our best people. But, even when people accept that things take time, they can still underestimate the amount of effort required. They may accept that it can take months to check and correct the bills of material file, for example, but how many people will that take? One CEO told me that his complete stock master file was going to be manually keyed into the new system by one person over a weekend: basic mathematics should have told him that this was impossible.

The problem is that, when tasks are unrealistically resourced, timescales get threatened and things get rushed. When things get rushed, people take inadvisable short-cuts and things don't get checked. The result is bad data in the system and no system performs well with bad data.

10.3.4 Over-estimating what the new system can do.

MRPII systems cost a lot of money. It is relative, of course, but for a small company £25,000 for a small system can be a lot of money. Even in large systems, hands must tremble when the pen hovers over a cheque for millions. It is easy, then, to believe that the new system will solve all of the company's problems. It won't.

At its simplest, you could say that MRPII identifies problems but people fix them. That is too simple, though. MRPII is an immensely powerful tool that people can use to solve problems throughout the organisation but, even then, it can't do everything. What can't it do? Well, it can enable people to change but it can't change them. It can support business decisions but it can't make those decisions. Giving me a paint brush won't turn me into Leonardo DaVinci: I would still need skill, application and dedication. Giving your people an MRPII system won't overnight turn them into world beaters: they will still need skill, application and dedication.

Obviously if you have written a proper ITT/SOUR and measured competing software packages against it, there should be no surprises at go-live in terms of functionality but a system, however good it is, is not a substitute for good management. Neither will a new system do people's jobs for them. A new system will not sort out your bad people and underperforming departments: highlight them, yes, but fix them, no.

10.3.5 Parallel projects.

Companies that want to progress frequently want to progress in several areas simultaneously. Whether it is a deliberate philosophy of continuous improvement or a new CEO full of energy and ideas, ERP/MRPII may not be the only game in town. When this happens, management time and attention will be diluted and the project may find itself competing for limited resource; be that money, facilities or people. Even worse, individuals can find themselves working on more than one project simultaneously, especially in small companies. Only the most skilled individuals can ride more than one horse at a time.

The larger the company, the easier it is to run multiple projects in parallel but, if you are a small company, don't try it and, if you are a large company, think everything through before you stretch too far.

10.3.6 Poor go-live planning.

You've taken lots of good advice and you've done everything right but you can still fall at the last hurdle. Going live is not just a case of taking out the old system and turning on the new. There is everything from data load to new stationery to consider and, although you can expect support from your system supplier (who will have been there before and can be expected to know what is involved), ultimate responsibility lies with the project manager and the project sponsor.

We have, in the chapter on implementation, looked at what is required for a successful go-live and now the project room should have its walls covered with check-lists, all enthusiastically ticked-off. Successful implementations don't just happen: they are planned, checked, organised and checked again. In the sure and certain knowledge that a failed implementation can do serious and sometimes irreparable damage to the company, going live must be the result of a rational decision and not just because a pre-planned date on a calendar has been reached. It should not happen before a conference room pilot has been carried out and carried out successfully. Right up to the last minute, the project sponsor must resist all temptation to be emotionally attached to a date and must be prepared to stop the go-live if everything is not ready and has not been proven to be ready.

One essential piece of planning that is frequently neglected is a fall-back plan. At the point of go-live, everything should have been checked and checked again. Everything has been tried, tested and signed off so nothing should go wrong. But we have all heard of Murphy's' Law. It is understandably rare for anything to go wrong with a well planned and executed implementation, but are you sure that if you ignored just one piece of advice in this book you did so for good reason? If not, what is your plan to cope with the unexpected? Perhaps you took short-cuts or perhaps you skimped on consultancy and training. If so, you are about to take a gamble. How confident are you? Just be aware that the option of a return to the old system will seem like a carrot for those whose commitment to the new system is suspect.

Remember also that if you switch off the new system and return to the old, the chances of resurrecting the new system will be close to zero and a large sum of money will have been wasted.

So don't take a gamble with the company's future; or your reputation and career.

10.4 Data.

10.4.1 Transferring data from the old system.

Everybody knows the saying, 'Garbage in; garbage out' so why do so many MRPII systems *still* go live with garbage data? There are a number of reasons; number one of which is that so many of us like to take shortcuts. We see the mountain of data that the new system needs (everything from parts files and bills of material to customer and supplier files) and it really is a mountain. Then we look at all of the data in the old system and it seems such a good idea just to copy it over.

But what is the quality of the data in the old system? Do we have the following?

- Obsolete parts
- Duplicate parts

- Inaccurate data on the stock file, such as lead times, batch sizes etc
- Obsolete or inaccurate bills of material
- Customers and suppliers that we haven't dealt with in years
- Sales orders, purchase orders and works orders that were delivered short and which we just never got around to closing.

If so, why on earth would we want to copy that data into a new system? Just because it is easy? If your data volumes are genuinely, and I mean genuinely, so great that re-keying the data is not an option, then start today on a major exercise on data clean-up in your old system. We have mentioned earlier how to get your bills of material file accurate but let's look at the other areas now.

Your first problem is finding out just how inaccurate your data is and there is no easy way to accomplish this. In the stock file, we mentioned earlier that it can be useful to sort and print records by various criteria so that we have a better chance of spotting duplicates. Sometimes a sort on the description is useful whilst a sort on costs can also be a possibility. But what about the accuracy of the data in each record? Ideally we would check every record individually but that can be an enormous task.

But again; listing the data in a suitable sort order can help. Similar items are likely to have similar characteristics: such as delivery lead time, cost, and batch sizes. You will be amazed, when running your eye down data that has been printed in tabular format, just how many apparent discrepancies can be easily spotted very quickly. If you have a range of items with 20 day lead times, the 10 day lead time in the middle will really jump out at you. I used the phrase 'apparent discrepancies' very deliberately: exceptions to a pattern may be suspicious but they are not necessarily wrong. For that reason, a low-level clerk cannot be given carte blanche to change data without first checking with people who actually know.

When it comes to out-of-date customer and supplier files, an easy way to spot companies that you no longer trade with is to look at the date of your last transaction with them. Just be careful about deleting these people if their account shows a current balance as this needs to be properly written off in your accounts first. Likewise it should be easy to spot old sales, purchase and works orders that need closing out but, again, make sure first that there are no outstanding invoices or balances to mess up your accounts.

I have been talking here about deleting data that is no longer relevant but be aware that some systems will not allow records to be deleted if there are, for example, transactions in history files that relate to those records. In these circumstances you can use a spare field to hold a flag and then ensure, when transferring data, that records with an 'obsolete' flag are not copied.

An alternative to correcting data in you old system is to export it into spreadsheets and correct it there before transferring it to your new. This can make the sorting and re-sorting of data easy and also allows mass changes to be carried out. Just one word of warning, though: the data clean-up is going to take weeks, if not months, and during that time new records will most probably be added to your old system. That means that you are going to have to have routines and procedures in place to cope with new parts, new bills, new customers etc, so that these get accurately added to your spreadsheets at the same time as they are added to the old system, as you will be up-loading only the records that are in the spreadsheets and not doing a re-read from your old files.

Some people believe that the best way to handle the data load, particularly when moving from paper based systems, is to manually key it into spreadsheets and check and amend it there. This is generally futile as it is almost certainly no faster than keying directly into the new system and is generally more expensive as special routines may need to be written to upload the data. The other point to consider is that, if your people key a load of records into a spreadsheet, they will learn nothing about keying records into your new system and that is something that they will be doing regularly post go-live as new products and customers etc come along. It is never too early to get used to a new system.

Remember also, if transferring data from an old system, that it is rarely as easy as it seems. Field lengths in the two systems may not match (what happens if your old system has a 50-character part description and your new system only 40 characters?) and, more likely, because your new system is likely to have more functionality than your old one, there will be data that you want in your new system that just doesn't exist in your old one. How are you going to handle that? Are you going to load records with default values for people to manually check and amend later? Will that actually happen or will busy people think that near enough is good enough?

Whatever you do; remember that data accuracy is not about going into your files every time you change systems to weed out the garbage:

it is about preventing that garbage being there in the first place. Get the necessary procedures in place now to ensure that any new system doesn't slide into the same swamp of inaccurate data that your old one did.

10.4.2 Un-necessary data.

To an extent we have covered this already in the section 'Because it was there' but is a point worth reiterating. Your new system is likely to have loads of extra data fields for people to get excited about and the temptation will be to fill these fields. That is rather like finding a tool and then going in search of something to fix with it. I know of one world-famous company that found a use for every field on the stock record, including every single spare field that had been created by the software authors to allow for future development. Creating and entering that data took a long time, of course, but worse: a couple of years after go-live, they had a genuine need to hold extra data on the file but nowhere to put it. I know that future-proofing is not an exact science but leave yourself some leeway to allow for the unexpected.

Index